BIPOLAR LIFE

*50 years of battling
manic-depressive illness
did not stop me
from building a
60 million dollar bi*

Steve Millard

MORGAN JAMES PUBLISHING • NEW YORK

BIPOLAR LIFE

ISBN: 978-1-60037-816-4 (Paperback)
Library of Congress Control Number: 2010930253

Published by:
MORGAN JAMES PUBLISHING
1225 Franklin Ave Ste 32
Garden City, NY 11530-1693
Toll Free 800-485-4943
www.MorganJamesPublishing.com

Cover/Interior Design by:
Rachel Lopez
rachel@r2cdesign.com

In an effort to support local communities, raise awareness and funds, Morgan James Publishing donates one percent of all book sales for the life of each book to Habitat for Humanity. Get involved today, visit **www.HelpHabitatForHumanity.org**.

DEDICATION

DEDICATION

This book is dedicated to my close friends who have helped me during the worst of times, Alan and Jean Yassky and Dave and Polly Henderson.

A very special thanks to Geoffrey Norman whose editorial skills made this book possible.

INTRODUCTION

INTRODUCTION

The pistol was a German Lugar, one of thousands that had made it back from Europe to the United States as a war souvenir. I'd bought it from someone, probably thinking that it would be handy around the house for protection and because I had always been something of a collector. It had been an impulsive purchase and I was doing a lot of impulsive things during those days. This night, I had taken the pistol with me when I walked down to the edge of a little pond not far from the house where I lived. I was going to use the Lugar to kill myself.

I had been drinking heavily all evening but my decision was not something I had suddenly come to in a state of drunkenness. Suicide had been on my mind, almost constantly, for days and maybe for weeks. Ever since I had come down off a long, psychotic high when I had felt invulnerable, even immortal, and had taken to calling myself "the Redeemer." That had gone on for months and during that time, I had been euphoric. I believed I could do anything. I seldom slept and when I did, it was never for more than three or four hours. During my waking hours, I was agitated, energized, and virtually consumed with ideas and schemes, most of them wildly impractical. I was arrogant and antagonistic to my co-workers. Impossible to my friends. I spent money recklessly and impulsively. I drank, not to medicate myself or to sooth the demons, but to fuel them.

Then…the crash. High as I had been for those months, I was now that low and, perhaps, even lower. This was depression of a kind I had not known was possible; of a kind that I didn't believe it possible to endure. It was not "the blues," or "the blahs" or the kind of melancholy that we all experience and learn to accept as part of life. This depression was not an emotional state but a physical condition. Every part of me suffered and cried out for some kind of relief. I was seldom able to sleep and when I did manage it for a few hours, I would wake up feeling beyond tired; feeling a sense of utter physical exhaustion. I had no appetite and when I did eat, there was no pleasure in it. I could barely taste the food. Alcohol brought no relief, only a temporary numbing of the pain which returned, and with more force, when the anesthesia wore off. The friends who had stood by during the wild, manic time tried to help but it seemed as though they existed somewhere out there, beyond my reach. I was alone and I was in pain.

So that night I tried, as I usually did, to numb the pain with alcohol but it didn't work. It almost never did. In the months before my crash, when I'd been on an ebullient high, I would drink without getting drunk, feeling ever more confident, sure of myself, and invulnerable with each round. Now, each drink seemed to make the layer of gloom around me thicker and more oppressive. This night, the alcohol would not even push me, unwilling, into sleep. I was wide-awake and more in agony than ever.

I could not imagine that I would ever break out of this deep depression; that the pain would ever stop. Depression, by definition, strips you of hope and the only thing to hope for, in my condition, was relief. I couldn't imagine that I would get better; that my torment would end. The only means I could see to end it was by killing myself.

So I took the Lugar and stepped out of the little house where I lived and into the night. It was after midnight but the pond was only fifty yards off and I knew the way. When I reached the bank, I sat down, held the pistol in front of my face, and jacked a round into the chamber. It would, I thought, be *so easy and so quick*. And it would be an end to the depression I believed would never end any other way. One pull of the trigger and I would be free of this agony. I wasn't anxious or afraid. Only a bit relieved. It was going to be all over.

I put the muzzle of the pistol to my right temple. Then ... I hesitated. And I thought, suddenly, "I'm too tough to do this."

I do not know, to this day, if it was a lack of courage or an inner strength that made me decide—firmly and conclusively—*not* to pull that trigger. I'll never know, I suppose, and in the end, maybe it was some of both.

In any case, I stood up and took a deep breath. I felt like I had been suffocating.

Then, I released the magazine from the pistol and ejected the shell from the chamber. I threw all the bullets in the pond but held on to the Lugar. Too cheap, I guess, to let it go after I'd paid good money for it. And a sign, maybe, that I hadn't given up entirely on the future.

The next day I took the Lugar to an auto-body shop and paid the man there to disable the pistol with a weld in the barrel. I still have that Lugar and I have looked at it many times as a reminder of how deep I had gone into darkness and how far, even on my worst day, I have come since then.

While I didn't destroy myself that night, the decision to keep on living did not mean that the depression was suddenly lifted and that I was no longer suffering its oppressive symptoms. The disease with which I was—and am—afflicted doesn't work that way. It is not that easy. I had passed through some kind of acute crisis but I was still not "cured," and I never will be.

By deciding, that night, to continue living, I had committed myself to living with and struggling with this disease. There was no escaping it. It was up to me to find ways to cope and to prevail over the disease and for the next twenty years or so, I would do that on my own, without medication and without professional help and, at first, without knowing, even, what the disease was called.

Learning to cope—especially during those years before medication and treatment—was a long process of self-education and self-help. It was a time of trial and error and of making the same mistakes that triggered attacks over and over until I learned to recognize symptoms and to avoid those behaviors that brought on attacks.

The disease, then, was a dominant factor in my life. But it was not my entire life and one of the prime reasons that I was determined to prevail in my struggle with the disease is that I was ambitious. I wanted to succeed in in life. For me, that meant succeeding in business and I couldn't do that unless I fought the disease that had almost taken me out entirely.

As I write, it has been nearly 50 years since that night. During those years, I struggled—and learned to cope—with my disease and I made my way up the ladder of success in business. In the beginning, I worked for others. First at the *Reader's Digest*, one of the largest and most recognizable American corporations, then for a small, start-up that became one of the great business success stories of the 1980's. And, finally, for myself, going out on my own with no money to speak of and financing my first year by selling some of the things I had collected and some property I had bought. I had no other backing and, when I started, no employees and only two clients. But I was a risk taker and I believed, perhaps irrationally, that I could handle the challenges of business the same way I had learned to handle my disease.

I ran my own company for 20 years and my client list included some of the most prestigious names in American business: Land's End, Williams-Sonoma, L.L. Bean, Ovis, and others. I turned my company over, eventually, to my employees, and retired to do more of the things I enjoy.

Now, with time on my hands, I think back about all that has happened since that night, when I sat next to the pond with that Lugar in my hand, calmly ready to pull the trigger. There was so much that I didn't know, then, and that I have learned since.

The lessons did not always come easy. Some came damned hard. But each lesson learned helped me develop mechanisms for dealing with the next challenge. The sum of all these lessons has made it possible for me to make a kind of truce with my condition. To experience a kind of peace that I would have never thought possible. Certainly not on the occasion when I stepped out into the night with a Lugar in my hand, fully intending to destroy myself. And not on many other, less intense occasions before and since.

But now that I have come to that place of relative peace—despite regular periods of depression—I feel a new kind of restlessness. It is an urge to share my experience and to pass along some of what I have learned. The obvious—and vain—way to account for this is to say I feel an obligation to help others and, in a sense, I do. But none of us operate from totally charitable and noble motives. And, in truth, there is the usual amount of human vanity in my desire to tell my story. We all go through life silently saying to the world, "Hey, look at me." But I do honestly believe I have a story to tell. If that is vanity, then so be it.

Also, I am a communicator. That is how I made my living and achieved a fair amount of success in business. I helped people in a certain sector of American business tell their stories to their customers. And I was (vanity, again) damned good at it. Good enough that my company had a wide reputation for integrity in an industry that wasn't known for that. I made sure we kept that reputation, no matter the cost. And it paid off. I am now quite comfortably retired with homes in the hills of New Hampshire where I live from May until October and on the coast of South Carolina where I spend the winter. I travel and I enjoy the good life which I believe, quite honestly, that I have earned.

But I am what I am, and I still feel this restless urge to communicate. Since I have no clients in my retirement, what I now have left to communicate is my own story. And I believe there is an audience for that story in the same way there were customers for my clients' stories when I was still in business.

We all say that we would like to help others and that may even be true. I know that, in my case, I owe an unrepayable debt to the people who helped me in the blackest times. So when I say that one reason I want to tell my story is that it would help others, I am talking about giving back in a real sense. In my long struggle with bi-polar illness, I had to educate myself about the disease if I was to have any hope of coping with it. When I first began exhibiting symptoms, the medical fraternity was not yet using the term "bi-polar." There has been a lot of progress since then, along a very steep learning curve. Like the experts and the specialists, I have learned a lot. By experience, trial and error, and study.

Among the many things I have learned—and one of the most emotionally arresting—is that I am not alone. One of the most painful aspects of any mental or emotional disease is that, when you are in its grip, you feel utterly alone, as though you cannot escape from the prison of your own suffering and, also, that no one can get inside to help.

But in my reading—and I have read widely about bi-polar—I came across this startling number:

Almost 16 million American adults experience bi-polar disorder.

I was struck by that number, I'm certain, because I thought that if my condition wasn't unique, then it was certainly rare. When I first realized that I suffered from a mental illness, I felt both fear and shame. The fear, for obvious reasons. The shame because I grew up thinking that people like that were freaks. Mental illness would not have been so stigmatizing, back then, if it had been considered commonplace. To be a freak, you have to be part of a very tiny minority.

Sixteen million American adults represents three percent of the population. Not a vast voting block, certainly; but not a tiny little minority, either. And many, many more than I would have guessed.

When I thought further about that number, it occurred to me that those sixteen million are not the only people who feel the impact and the effects of bi-polar disorder. Those sixteen million have families and friends for whom the disease is as baffling and heartbreaking as it is for the patients themselves. And they do not have physicians treating them; nor are there medications to help them in their struggles. In some ways, the condition is more mysterious and sinister for them than it is for the actual patient who at least experiences the symptoms of his condition first hand. His loved ones merely have his mysterious and troubling behavior to go on.

I don't know the actual number of people who feel directly the effects of bi-polar disorder. Pointless, even, to guess. But the number is large and I often find myself thinking about those people and what they go through. I hope that some of them will read this book and that it will comfort them to know that they are not alone and that there are strategies for coping with their condition and, even, beating it. Not in the sense of making it go away or even destroying it. That won't happen. But beating it in the sense that it no longer rules their lives and limits their chances for success and happiness.

One of my doctors (you will learn more about him later in this book) has remarked, to me and to others, that he has been inspired by my "pragmatic" approach to dealing with bi-polar disorder. I'm flattered, I suppose. But, then, I don't know how else I might have dealt with it. The condition was—*is*—a fact. And facts are things you can ignore, change, or deal with. The first two options were not available to me. I took the third, by elimination.

How did I deal with the fact of my bi-polar disorder? Well, in many ways that is the subject of this book. Some of the steps I took seem obvious. Like, for instance, getting that weld put in the barrel of the Lugar so I couldn't use it to blow my brains out the next time I went into severe depression. Others I learned through painful trial and error. Many from wise physicians and other sufferers. It was a long and arduous process of education which still goes on. "Know thyself," the ancient Greeks wisely counseled. In my case, there did not seem any other option. I would either know myself—and, thus, how to manage that sometimes unruly self—or I would cease to be a self. So I have learned. Not all there is to know, certainly. But some of it. And, perhaps, much of it. Enough that I feel the old communicator's urge to shape it into a form that will find an audience that will find what I have to say compelling and useful. That audience includes, of course, those sixteen million bi-polar patients and their families. And, also, those who are not sufferers but merely travelers on a road that they hope will take them to success in business. Mine came both despite and because of my condition. I learned a lot about business while I was learning about myself and my bi-polar disorder. I'm happy to share that knowledge, too.

Stephen Millard
Peterborough, New Hampshire

TABLE OF CONTENTS

TABLE OF CONTENTS

CHAPTER 1

CHAPTER 1

S tart at the beginning. The beginning of my struggles with bipolar disorder, that is. For most patients, the disease appears when they are in their 20s and I hit it right about on the money. I was 27 and if you'd asked me, I would have told you I didn't have a care in the world. I was living in Hawaii, making good money, and doing challenging work that I liked. I was single and I went out almost every night and I met a lot of women.

I found myself living this life through a series of accidents and lucky breaks and a certain element of hard work and determination on my part. When I was in college at the University of Vermont, I was in Air Force ROTC and it kept me in school. The courses that were part of the program were the only elements in the curriculum that genuinely interested me and that I really did well in. For the rest of it, I did what I needed to do to get by and I enjoyed the college life. A friend of mine at UVM named Alan Yassky, who later helped pull me out of the depths, once told someone that the way he remembered me from those days was as "the life of the party, a guy who was always singing or tap dancing or somehow on stage."

I can't argue with him.

But I was serious about Air Force ROTC. I was going to be a fighter pilot. It was something I had wanted since I was a boy and I was determined to make it happen. So I worked hard on the ROTC classes and I performed well at summer camp and I was sure, when I graduated and got my commission as a 2nd lieutenant, that I would be going to flight school and on to an operational fighter squadron. This was 1957, in between Korea and Vietnam and the Air Force could afford to be very selective. But I wasn't worried. I knew I would do whatever it took.

But I had not factored in a very minor defect in my vision. It came up in the first time I took something called the "red lens" test. I had passed a flight physical when I was still in college so this caught me completely by surprise when I was tested again, after I'd been commissioned. I couldn't believe it and asked for a re-test. I failed this one, too. Failure meant that I was disqualified from going to flight school. So I asked for yet another re-test. And then another, until I had taken—and failed—the test 9 times. That's when the flight surgeon called me into his office and said, "Lieutenant, I don't want to hear about you requesting another re-test and, in fact, if a plane flies over and I even see you look up, I'll have you court martialed."

It was the end of my dream of becoming a fighter pilot and I still think about that with a certain regret.

Well, if I couldn't fly fighters, I would do the next best thing. I went to Tyndall Air Force Base in Florida to fighter control school. It was demanding and on a couple of occasions, I found the stress almost too much. But it was also exhilarating to be at the radar screen, watching those blips and knowing that they were real airplanes being flown by real pilots at what seemed like unbelievable speeds. If you made a mistake, some of the planes on your scope might collide with each other or fly into the ground or not make it back to base because you'd sent them too far out and they didn't have the fuel it took to get back. You had to make very quick decisions and they had to be right. You had to be confident in your decisions and that had to come through over the radio to the guy who was in the cockpit.

It was pressure-cooker work and once I got the hang of it, I became very good at it and I came to love it.

My first real duty assignment as a fighter controller was to a forlorn little island about one mile by two miles that sat halfway between Korea and Japan. It was called Mishimi and it was bleak and inhospitable in the extreme. But the work was very challenging and exciting. This was, in a way, the very front line of the cold war. Like Berlin, only on the other side of the world. We'd send up our planes—mostly F-86Ds—and we could look at the scope and see the Migs coming up from Korea to tease them without taking it to the point of an actual engagement.

On one occasion, when we were training Japanese pilots we had a flight of three F-86s that were being flown by Japanese pilots and the rockets in the nose of the lead plane malfunctioned and it just blew up. The pilot ejected and we were able to calculate the speed and direction of the winds aloft and calculate the drift and get the boats out to rescue the guy. But the other two pilots just came unglued and were screaming in Japanese over the radio and flying further apart, on courses that could make real trouble both for getting them back and also getting them into the wrong airspace.

I started talking to them, as patiently as I could, using the one or two words of Japanese that I knew and slowly getting them back into the little bit of English that they knew. I also got some help from my Japanese supervisor, who had been so excited, at first, that he lost his command of English. But I got him settled down. Then we got the pilots settled down and eventually, and everyone started responding to my directions and we got those planes back to base. But it had been some very harrowing minutes that seemed like hours.

I got a commendation for that.

I bring all that up, not so much to blow my own horn (even though that is always fun) but to make the point that while I was only a couple of years from the onset of a severe, clinical mental illness, I was not merely functional but highly functional. I was not someone who sat in a room, fearful and anxious and unable to go out and make it in the world. I was not that, at all. I was an Air Force officer doing important work in a high-pressure environment and doing it very well, if I do say so. Furthermore, I loved it. If you'd asked me, back then, if I considered myself distressed or disturbed, I would have thought that *you* were the one who was crazy.

Me? Depressed? Disturbed? Hell no. I was fine. Top of the world.

And I was still feeling that way after three years of active duty, when I went on reserve status and took a job with the National Guard in Hawaii. I was still a fighter director but was being paid as a civilian government employee. As a GS 14, I was making something like $15,000 a year which was actually great money for a single man in those days. In Hawaii, I was assigned to the northern island of Kuai and I was training the Guardsmen there to control fighters. I worked about 10 days out of every month. It was a very sweet deal.

And I was still on top of my game as a fighter director. There was one incident that I'll never forget when a Marine Corps pilot in what was called an F-8-U, or a Crusader, ran into trouble out over the ocean. The plane had gas tanks in each wing and when one tank ran out, the pilot switched over the other. But in this case there was an equipment malfunction and the pilot couldn't get fuel over to the tank that was running dry from the one that was still full. He radioed in a "Mayday," and we went to work trying to figure something out.

The pilot was, understandably, nervous. Maybe even a little worse than that. He didn't want to bail out if he didn't have to, but he didn't want to flame- out on approach when he might be too low and have too little airspeed to make the end of a runway. I started talking to him while I looked for the closest airstrip and made the calculations about how long he could keep flying. I found an old strip that had been built in World War II and had been abandoned. It was just barely long enough, I thought, for him to land the plane and get it stopped. So I called the pilot and told him I thought I could get him in there.

"Are you sure?" he said. His voice sounded like it had gone up a full octave.

"I'm sure," I said, "trust me." I was trying to get him calmed down so I made myself sound calm and utterly in control. But I wasn't actually all that sure. It was going to be close.

Well, I kept talking to him and talking to him and keeping him on the right heading and he made it onto final and landed safely. By now, that one gas tank was just about bone dry. It was a near thing. So near, in fact, that he flamed out just after his wheels hit the ground. The pilot was incredibly grateful and thought I was a hero. It was obvious that he had peed in his flight suit ... but who wouldn't have.

So I got a letter of commendation from the Air Force for my coolness and professionalism and all that. The truth is ... it could just as easily have been a court martial if that Marine pilot hadn't gotten that plane to the airstrip and had crashed into the ocean instead.

But I'd never thought that way. Never considered it. Like most young men, I thought I was invulnerable. Bulletproof. So I did my job at a high level of performance and when I wasn't doing my job, I was having fun.

Then I met—and fell in love with—an Hawaiian woman named Myrtle. She was both lovely and a good person and I could not believe my good fortune when, after I'd asked her to marry me, she said, "Yes."

The next morning, I woke up feeling frightened beyond words. It was a profound fear. The kind that makes your insides feel cold. Like the fear you feel when a vicious dog jumps out from somewhere, unexpectedly, and attacks you. Except that this fear would not go away or even fade a little. It was *constant*.

It had lasted for several days before I finally decided that I had to go to the hospital. I had no medical knowledge but for some reason—perhaps because of stories I'd heard military men tell—I thought I might have syphilis. The extent of what I knew about that disease was a) how you got it and b) that it could rot your brain. I'd lived a fairly wild life in Japan and Hawaii so there wasn't any question about having done what you did to get it. And, if I couldn't say that my brain was rotting, it was pretty clear that *something* was very badly wrong and the symptoms were not physical.

I needed help. If someone couldn't do something to help make things better then I wanted, at the very least, to know what was wrong. *Why* was I feeling this way? I was an optimistic person and a problem solver and I just wanted someone to tell me what was wrong and what do about it.

I had no idea how long I would have to wait for answers to those questions

CHAPTER 2

CHAPTER 2

I began looking for an answer—or answers—when I had that first attack, while I was still in my 20's, working in Hawaii, making what seemed like great money doing work I loved. I had a wonderful life that I had been enjoying to the fullest and then ... this unrelenting sense of alarm bordering on panic. It was a feeling that was probably described best by the novelist, William Styron, who suffered from depression and came out of it long enough to write a brilliant book before sinking back and never recovering. In *Darkness Visible*: Styron describes the physical symptoms of depression this way:

... gloom crowding in on me, a sense of dread and alienation and ... stifling anxiety.

I felt something like that, and what made it worse, if anything could, was that there was no widespread therapeutic language for my condition. People did not talk about "depression," as a clinical condition and the term "bi-polar illness" was not part of the psychological vocabulary.

So I was flying blind, so to speak. And more than anything, I craved relief from the pain and distress I was experiencing. If that wasn't possible, I wanted—at the very least—to know what was causing this terrible sense of fear and anxiety. I hoped for a cure and would have been satisfied, I suppose, with an explanation.

So I went to the hospital where I described my symptoms. After a checkup and some routine tests, the diagnosis was … there was nothing physically wrong with me. I did not have syphilis or any other disease that would have accounted for my distress. I couldn't believe it. I knew that I wasn't imagining my own symptoms and, plainly, the people in the hospital agreed because they suggested, very strongly, that I visit the hospital in Honolulu where they had an outpatient psychiatric facility.

At first, I didn't want to go. Or, rather, I didn't want to believe that it was even possible that I *needed* to go. I was in complete denial when it came to mental illness. *Not me*, I thought. It couldn't be. I was an officer in the Air Force; a skilled fighter controller with commendations to prove it. I had performed under stress, again and again. How could I possibly need to see a psychiatrist?

But eventually I went to Honolulu and the hospital there and that was, I think, clear evidence of just how severely distressed I was and now desperate I was for some help.

I couldn't accept that I was ill in *that* way … but I went just the same.

Since I was on outpatient status at the hospital, I stayed in downtown Honolulu at a cheap and depressing little hotel. My room had no window and to get away, I would go to a movie theatre and sit through two or three showings of the same film. Then I would go to a bar and drink alone. In the morning, I would get up and go to the hospital where I was seen by a psychiatrist, a man who was trained in the Freudian theories that were prevalent at the time.

He asked me what I thought were inane questions and I barely paid attention to them or to the answers I gave him. I had no confidence in the man, perhaps because early in our conversations, I noticed that he always seemed to be wearing one brown and one black sock. Those mismatched socks are just about all that I remember from those sessions. And they were, I think, the only thing that made any real impression on me. I was confused and in denial and taking some very strong drugs that the psychiatrist had prescribed. It was as though I was sleepwalking through the entire experience, unaware of almost everything that was going on around me except for those mismatched socks.

Finally, after more than a week of this, I told the man that I had an important job and that I needed to get back to it. Which was true. But it was also true that I wanted to get away from him and the depressing routine I had fallen into.

The psychiatrist said that he didn't think it was a good idea for me to leave; that I needed more help. I wasn't interested but I did ask him for his diagnosis.

He told me I was schizophrenic.

I'm not sure I had ever heard that term before. If I had, it hadn't made an impression. When that doctor used that word to account for what was wrong with me, I certainly did not know what it meant or the terrible condition it described. But I wanted to find out, so when I was back at my job, I went to the library and did some research. I looked up the word in the encyclopedia and what I learned was truly terrifying. I read the entry in the encyclopedia and I was stunned. My insides felt like they had turned to water. If that psychiatrist's diagnosis was correct, then I was lost. There was no cure, no hope, no prospect of anything other than madness and dementia and an end in some grim asylum.

At this point I did two things: I went into a deeper kind of denial and concealment. I couldn't bear to think about what I believed to be my condition and what it meant for my future and I was petrified by the prospect that someone— anyone—might find out.

And ... I tearfully broke off the engagement to Myrtle. I couldn't imagine asking anyone to share what I thought of as my fate. And I tried to bury the knowledge of my condition as deep as possible. As a way of doing this, I went back to instructing the Hawaii National Guard crews in fighter control techniques. I threw myself into my work, and I gradually began to feel better. As I learned much later, the mind will eventually mend itself and that knowledge has been priceless.

But that was much later in my life. When I was healing after that first episode, I deliberately avoided thinking very much about my illness. Denial was my only strategy and the healing made it easier to pretend that nothing had happened or, if it had, that it was some kind of accident that wouldn't happen again. Better not to think about it. Better to get on with life.

So that is what I did … keeping my secret from others as well as from myself.

CHAPTER 3

CHAPTER 3

Things were not the same after that first episode. But, then, how could they be? I was in denial, as I say, but no matter how deeply I buried my secret, I still *knew*. I not only carried with me the memory of the experience itself, but I had heard that terrible word, *schizophrenia*, applied to me and my condition. And after that session in the library, I knew, indelibly, what that word meant.

So everything was different. My whole world had come apart.

Still, here I was. Alive. With a job to do. Responsibilities. People who depended on me. Friends.

Like they say, life goes on, so I got on with my life. I went back to work and I did my job. Then, even though I was offered a chance to stay on, at the end of my one-year contract with the Hawaii Air National Guard, I decided to pack it up and go back home.

All these years later, when I look back on that decision, I am of two minds about it. The decision seems both perfectly understandable and completely inexplicable.

Until my breakdown (if that is the right word), I was having the time of my life. I was being paid more, I'm certain, than I could have expected to make if I'd quit and looked for a job in the civilian world.

I lived a very pleasant life in Hawaii. I had a house on the beach and a car I liked—a '55 Chevy—and enough money to go out whenever I wanted. I was single and, until the heartbreak with Myrtle, I was meeting and spending time with a lot of women. I would be hard to imagine a better, more agreeable life for a young bachelor of those times.

Still … even before my breakdown (and I'm not sure how much it influenced my decision) I had assumed I would leave Hawaii at the end of my contract. The question, I suppose, is *why*.

The answer, I think, is that I just assumed that I was going to go work and find my calling somewhere in the world of American business and that I was going to succeed. I don't want to sound too grand, here, and imply that I felt like I was destined to do great things or something like that. But I did believe I was going to find something, work hard at it, and get ahead. Like most people back then, I was ambitious. I didn't think there was anything wrong with that and I still don't. I was mentally and emotionally programmed for success even if I didn't know, yet, what I would succeed at doing.

My purpose in writing this book—part of it, anyway—is to pass along what I have learned about two things: dealing with bi-polar disorder and succeeding in business. These may seem like wildly separate—or even contradictory—themes but I believe they are related. I *know* that this has been true in my life. I'm not sure that I would have succeeded in business if I had not been bi-polar. I know that sounds odd but I think my meaning will become clear, later on, as I continue with my story.

I am far more certain that I would not have been able to successfully cope with my bi-polar condition if I had not first learned to deal with the challenges of business. If, that is, I had not been conditioned—by a lifetime of working and making a living—to facing challenges and figuring out how to deal with them. I imagine that if I had been an artist of some sort, that I might have suffered the same kind of fate that of so many solitary and talented bi-polar people.

But being someone who was accustomed to working at a job, I usually felt like I had responsibilities and that people depended on me. Even when I was, much later, suffering from the depression—the "down" cycle of bi-polar—I would feel this need to get up and go do what was expected of me. That sense of responsibility helped me from feeling totally alone in my struggles.

You feel alone and helpless when you are suffering from depression—that is, when you are in the "down" phase of the manic/depressive cycle. You feel like you can't be helped. That even if you could be helped ... nobody would want to help you because you aren't worth the effort.

And, of course, you can't be helped if you feel this way and if you aren't willing to make some effort to help yourself. It can be done—as I have spent a lifetime learning—but it is hard work and you have to make yourself do it. And keep doing it. Even though the payoff may seem non-existent at first and a long, long way off after that. Too far off, you think, to be worth the effort. But you have to make it anyway. You have to keep working. And that is the oldest, most reliable way to succeed in business, too. You work hard, keep working, and you try not to let the setbacks keep you down. You develop a habit of doing what you know you have to do even when you don't especially want to do it.

So, getting back to my decision to leave my very agreeable life in Hawaii and head back to the mainland and an uncertain future ... I'm sure that I would never have taken the risk if I had not been accustomed to working and working hard. I *believed* that I would succeed even though I didn't even have a job lined up. I had sent out a few letters to the personnel departments at big companies like 3M but I hadn't heard anything back. Still, I wasn't discouraged and it never occurred to me that I would go back and fail. I was sure I would find a job because I always had. I had been finding jobs, after all, since I was 9 years old.

I started out my long career in business as a sole proprietor—collecting empty bottles for deposit. It doesn't sound like much but you could get 2 cents for a small bottle and 5 cents for the larger ones and for a 9-year-old kid back then, that was real money. After all, a candy bar cost a nickel. I don't think the deposit on a returnable bottle has gone up at all but the price of a candy bar is now a lot more than a nickel.

I moved up to raking leaves after a while and that's when I learned my first great lesson of business. Early on in this new career, I had taken on what I would now think of as a "client." She was a very sweet old woman who had a yard that was just covered with leaves. She needed them raked up and hauled off and couldn't do it herself so I took on the job. I worked very hard and it took me all day and when I was finished and went to the door, the woman looked out at the yard, told me I had done a marvelous job, thanked me profusely, and gave me 2 pennies and a peach. I could have made as much if I had found one bottle and taken it in for the deposit.

I was young. But not too young to learn a lesson that stayed with me for life. I never took on any project unless I knew, very clearly, what the deal was. I never raked another lawn for 2 cents with a bonus of a peach for good work.

A couple of years after that, I took on a paper route. It was a seven-days-a-week job with Sundays being the worst day. I used my bike for daily papers but had to haul the Sunday editions around in a wagon. I kept that job for several years; until I was still in junior high school when I got a job taking newspapers off the press and bundling them for delivery. I had this job even while I was playing football and I remember coming to practice with the ink from those newspapers all over my clothes. My mother made a special apron for me to keep my clothes clean.

Then, there was the job I had picking strawberries. It was hard work; stoop labor, and the man who owned the strawberry farm paid me 10 cents for every one of those pint baskets I'd fill. I noticed, then, that strawberries were selling for 50 cents at the market. So I went to the man who owned the strawberry patch and asked him what his price to me would be for a package of strawberries that I'd picked. He said 20 cents, which meant I picked the strawberries and paid him 10 cents on top of my labor.

So, I picked a crate of strawberries, paid him the difference between by labor and his price, and got on my bike. I rode around my neighborhood, knocking on doors, selling strawberries for the market price. Only you didn't have to go to the market to buy them. So you were getting free delivery and the strawberries were fresh, straight from the farm.

I did that all through that strawberry season and I learned something else— and this may have been the first hint that I might be something of a salesman. I noticed that if I went home and cleaned up—showered and changed out of my dirty strawberry-picking clothes—that I had more trouble moving product than if I just went straight from the strawberry farm. Something about those dirty clothes and the strawberry juice that was still on my fingers and my t-shirt must have convinced my customers that they were getting *really* fresh product. And they were. It wasn't a gimmick ... or maybe it was. But it wasn't a *lie*. It was a way of accentuating the truth. When you are selling, you need to go with your strengths. It seems obvious, but it also seems obvious that if you are selling product door to door, you should arrive looking clean and presentable.

Depends on the product. Depends on what you are selling.

Anyway. I moved on from strawberries to picking tobacco. My family was living in Connecticut by this time and I was 14 years old. There is a lot of tobacco grown along the Connecticut River valley. It is the variety that is used in cigar wrappers. It has to be picked by hand and it is hard work. You are outside, under a hot sun, with insects biting you. They pay immigrants to do the work these days. When I did it, they paid me 40 cents an hour.

The tobacco leaves were sorted and stacked in piles and then these tractors with forklifts were used to move the piles around. I was talking to one of the tractor drivers one day and he told me he made 80 cents an hour. Twice the money I was making and he didn't have to bend over or get down on his knees in the dirt. I didn't know how to drive a tractor and wasn't old enough to get a driver's license. I couldn't do anything about being young but I figured I could learn how to drive a tractor. How hard could it be? So I asked one of the hands to show me and after a while, I had the hang of it. Then, one day, the call went out for someone who knew how to drive a tractor and I volunteered. The boss wasn't sure at first but once he saw that I knew what I was doing, I was a tractor driver. I had a promotion and I'd doubled my salary. I was like moving from the bullpen to the corner office.

The lessons from that one were pretty obvious. You need to keep improving yourself and learning new skills. That's how you get out of the hot sun and into the shade of the warehouse, driving a tractor and making the big money.

I held down those jobs, and others, when I was in junior-high and high school. I worked year-round, right through the winter, and on weekends and never thought there was anything unusual or onerous about it. I liked to work and I liked to make money, even though I wasn't much of a consumer. Or, not much of a *shopper* anyway. There were things I wanted and that I spent my money on but they were collectables. Especially stamps. I began stamp collecting when I was young and later on, I branched out into art and fine guns and historical artifacts. I don't claim to understand the psychology of this but maybe there was some kind of link, in my mind, between hard work and the satisfactions of owning something that isn't perishable and maybe even increases in value. Some of those stamps I bought with strawberry and tobacco picking money have become quite valuable. So maybe, even then, I was learning not just about making money but also about its value. About investing.

Whatever I might have been learning, I was too young and too busy to give it much though. I was just working. It didn't get in the way of school or sports.

I loved sports and I played with the kind of intensity that comes from having a passion for the game. I went a lot further on desire than I did on talent. Or size. At 119 pounds, I was the smallest player on my high school football team. But because I was the second fastest guy on the team, they put me in the defensive backfield. At safety. The fastest player on the team was one of our halfbacks and the coaches didn't want him to get hurt tackling people while he was playing defense. Apparently, I was expendable.

I also played 3rd string quarterback, although I was terrible at it. A lot of that could be blamed on my size. At 5 feet, 4 inches, I had a hard time seeing over the defensive linemen and spotting receivers downfield.

This, of course, totally eliminated my passing game. But I was good at hiding the ball and slipping around end, because the defensive linemen couldn't see me, either.

But if I wasn't much on offense, I really loved playing safety and making the hits on ball carriers. I would tackle them right at shoe-top level and they almost always came right down. Even the big, lumbering giants.

My football career even came to the attention of the local papers and I was written up a couple of times. One story mentioned that I was "… the lad who won the town marble shooting championship two years ago." The story also noted that I was, at 119 pounds, the smallest member of the varsity.

Tennis was my other big sport. I taught myself to play at the elementary school playground near my house. I drew a chalk line a wall, at the height of the net, and I would hit the ball for hours. Still, I didn't make the team my freshman year of high school, so I hit the ball some more—a lot more—and I made the team sophomore year.

I played third singles and won all my matches when we played the other large Connecticut high schools. My most memorable match was when we played West Hartford, the snobbiest school in the state.

My opponent was a classic tennis brat who had obviously spent half his life on the court, being tutored in the fine points of the game. I was self-taught and there wasn't much style to my game. But I was fast and could cover the court so I returned almost everything. Which frustrated my opponent mightily.

The match came down to a contest of class *vs.* determination. Which means—he far outclassed me but I hit everything back to him. This finally got to him and he began making mistakes and, eventually, I won. When my opponent came to the net, he threw his racquet at me like it was a bolo. I ducked, jumped the net, and punched him in the face.

Not a stylish, Wimbleton sort of ending but a great moment—and memory—for me.

Well, as you can gather, I was a lot better athlete than I was a student. My time went to sports and to my jobs and when I graduated from high-school and went to college, that didn't change. I kept right on working.

During the school year, I sold sandwiches in the girls' dorms. I had a car I'd bought with $400 of the money I'd saved from my paper route, years before. It was a '49 Chevy and a lousy car but if I remembered to put a quart of oil in it every few blocks, it got me around campus so I could work that sandwich-selling operation.

One summer vacation, I worked as a bartender at a resort in Lake George, New York. I learned the lesson all bartenders learn—how to be nice to customers you'd like to punch in the nose, or at least tell to shut up and go home, anyway. I remember this veteran bartender asking me, "Kid, how much you hit the till for?" He explained how it was done and that all bartenders did it. But I couldn't. While I had a kind of natural inclination to make money, I wasn't interested in stealing it.

So, in short, I knew how to work and make money and when I returned to the mainland four years after I'd graduated from college, I had no reason to think I'd lost that ability. I just assumed that once I got back and started looking around, I'd find something and I'd work hard at it and I would succeed.

The big question, the imponderable in my life, was this new thing that had sent me to a hospital where I was told I suffered from a terrifying and incurable mental condition. That I was—I could hardly make myself say, or even think, the word—*schizophrenic*. Like I say, the only way I could deal with this was to bury it inside and deny.

So far, I had learned a lot about work and making money and selling and getting ahead and all of that would prove to be invaluable over the years.

But I had a much tougher education ahead of me and many, many hard lessons to learn when it came to dealing with that other thing.

And no choice but to learn them.

CHAPTER 4

CHAPTER 4

After a long and liquid going-away party, some friends poured me on an airplane and I left Hawaii. I slept all the way to Chicago and then I made my way to Detroit where I bought a car. I suppose I thought I'd get a good deal on the car if I bought it there. Turned out the car was a piece of junk. It was a '59 Ford Fairlane and you'd dent the fenders if you touched them too hard. Every time I drove that car, I missed the Chevy back in Hawaii. And, I suppose, there were a lot of times when I missed the rest of the life I'd left back there, too.

But it doesn't do any good to look back so I moved on.

Since I didn't have a job—or a plan, for that matter—I took my old college roommate up on an offer to come live with him while I looked around and settled on my next move.

He was a lawyer and he had a job in Washington, D.C., working in the office of a congressman from Connecticut. We found a place in the Cardinal House Apartments just across the river in Arlington. I had saved money while I was in Hawaii so I bought all the furniture. It was cheap Danish-modern but good enough for a couple of young bachelors. The building was fine and we had good neighbors, including Ted Sorenson who became famous a couple of years later as a speechwriter and advisor to President John F.

Kennedy. I would run into Sorenson in the hall or the elevator now and then, and he was always polite.

I needed a job and I started looking right away. The best I could do was a sales position with a company called Addressograph-Multigraph. They made a kind of deluxe mimeograph machine that fed the paper automatically when you plugged it in, instead of turning a crank by hand. Those machines were big back then but about to be made obsolete by Xerox copiers and other new technologies. My job was very mundane; I wasn't even selling the machines. Just the replacement ink and cartridges and other supplies. I hated it, in no small part because my boss was a former Air Force enlisted man who must have had trouble from officers because he still carried a grudge which he enjoyed taking out on me once he'd found out about my service.

Still, I was young and it was Washington which, just like now, was full of young, ambitious people who were out to conquer the world and, by the way, have a little fun while they are at it. So there were parties and I met women and had some good times.

But there were clouds on my horizon. I had these episodes where I would feel depressed or, worse, a glimmer of that sense of panic that had come over me for the first time in my life—and so overwhelmingly—when I was back in Hawaii. I tried to write it off as being caused by the job situation. Another form of the denial strategy, I suppose. But I knew that there was more to it and I was afraid.

But I couldn't tell anyone. Not my roommate and certainly not anyone at work. It was essential, I thought, that I keep my emotional problems—my *condition*—an absolute secret. *Nobody* could know.

That may require some explanation since we live in a time when people talk openly about almost everything. If you have a problem or a weakness, you are not supposed to be afraid to talk about it. In fact, these days people believe that *not* talking about something like alcoholism or emotional problems— things that would have been considered shameful not too many years ago— only makes those things worse. That it is a mistake to keep problems like that a secret and bottled up. That it just adds to the emotional stresses and burdens you live under.

And, certainly, I can understand that. Living with a secret that you consider shameful is no fun. It is hard; unremittingly hard. You don't get much time off from the worry and the dread that you will be found out. The secret is a like a weight that you carry around with you all the time and it doesn't get lighter the more practice you have carrying it.

So, I'm all for people being able to talk honestly and openly about things like—well, in my case, bi-polar illness. It is a lot easier dealing with the problem when you don't have to worry that somehow, someone might find out.

But I should add here that while this openness and honesty is undeniably a good thing, being able to talk about your condition does not mean that you are suddenly "cured." Simply being able to look someone in the eye and tell him, without shame, that you are bi-polar does not result in a parting of the heavens and a new day of pure, radiant sunshine. Openness might be necessary if you want to reach an accommodation with a condition like mine but it certainly isn't sufficient. Confession—or, perhaps, *candor*—does not end the struggle. I merely takes you a little further toward your goal. Which is the ability to live and function and enjoy the blessings of life in spite of your problem.

But … getting back to my story, letting people know—or find out—about my condition was unthinkable back when I was in Washington even though the secrecy was hard emotionally. These were the 50's (actually, the very early 60's) which we now remember as a time of dull conformity. This is a simplistic view, of course. But the 50's were not, certainly, what the later years of the 60's turned out to be and not like the way we live now.

Back then, most of the young people I knew wanted to be normal and successful. In fact, part of being normal *was* wanting to be successful. And, it was hard to be successful if you weren't "normal." So, I wanted to be normal. I *had* to be if I wanted to be successful and get along in life and that was what I wanted, maybe even more than other people.

But in those moments when I wasn't in denial, when I was face-to-face with the truth, I knew there was this problem and that it wasn't some small thing. I'd heard that awful word "schizophrenia" used to describe this mysterious condition that had come over me with such force when I was in Hawaii and that I would feel coming back, if not so violently, from time to time in Washington. It was something I did not want to think about and when I did think about it, I felt this kind of sick, lonesome fear. That feeling was bad enough. Being alone with it; not being able to confide in anyone and feel the reassurance of a few words of encouragement or sympathy … that made it worse.

But that was the world—the reality—I lived in.

There were two or three times during the year or so that I was in Washington, when the pressure and the sense of fear got to be too much and I did reach out for help as an outpatient at a local hospital. I saw a doctor on those visits and they did what they could to calm me down and reassure me. Which wasn't much. But even though I had to sneak around like a thief to make those visits, they did calm me down and make me feel a little better.

There were a couple of reasons for this, I suppose. First, it just helped to talk to somebody. Anybody. After holding it in so long, it felt like this pressure had been released, even if it was just a little. And it made me feel like I was doing *something*.

And I'd always liked to think of myself as someone who faced problems and dealt with them.

Still, most of the time I tried not to think about this other thing and to get on with my life. I met a woman and we started going out and then seeing each other exclusively and the more serious the thing between us got, the more I felt this sense of anxiety, bordering on dread. I didn't understand, then, what would become clear much later. There are "triggers," that bring on episodes or attacks when you have a condition like mine. Intimacy, it turns out, is a trigger for me.

But I was young, then, and in denial about my condition. I was also afraid. I laid a lot of my feelings of anxiety on my job and the fact that I hated it. It was an evasion, of course. Hating my job didn't make me unique or account for the terrible sense of anxiety I felt for what seemed like no reason at all. But it was easier and more comforting for me to think that it was my work and not this other, much larger and incomprehensible thing that accounted for my troubles.

That would have been too much to deal with, so I put the blame on my job.

And I quit.

CHAPTER 5

CHAPTER 5

I wasn't sure of my next move, once I'd quit my dreary Washington job. I needed to find something but I didn't have any leads. What I wanted to do, first of all, was get out of Washington. I had broken it off with the woman I'd been seeing and I was unemployed so there wasn't anything keeping me there. It was summer and that was the worst time to be in Washington even if everything else in your life was on-track and going well. And that hardly described the shape I was in.

So, I went up to a place my parents owned in the country, outside of Troy, New York. It was a rustic sort of place, kind of a cabin out in the woods. I moved in there and hung around without much to do except think about what I would do next … or, maybe, try *not* to think about that. Things had gotten off track in my life and I knew that fixing things, at least superficially, was a matter of finding a job and then throwing myself into my work. But there was that other thing—this problem that I couldn't share with anyone and that I couldn't even put a name to—and even when I could force myself *not* to think about it, I knew that it was there. So I felt this unfamiliar lassitude that made doing routine things seem either very hard or just pointless. I recognize it now as depression but back then … well, I didn't know.

I knew it wasn't fun and what I wanted was some relief, a way of escaping, and I found the means for that in these old copies of *Readers Digest*. There were dozens of them stacked up around the cabin. There was no television in the cabin and I'm not sure that if there had been, it would have been as distracting as those old issues of the *Readers Digest* that I went though, page after page. I enjoyed the jokes and the articles about life in America and the condensed best-selling books. I especially liked a feature called "Humor in Uniform," probably because I'd so recently gotten out of the Air Force and the little vignettes about service life took me back to a better, happier time.

That, actually, was what reading those old magazines did for me—they were a distraction from my depression. When I was reading them, I was absorbed in something besides my own troubles. And, then, I suppose you could say that those long voyages I took through those well-thumbed pages set me up for where I landed next.

There was a phone at the cabin but nobody called in and I wasn't calling out. Then, one day, the phone did ring and it startled me out of what I was usually doing—reading something in the *Reader's Digest*. The call was from my old roommate in Washington. He was a good friend and he was looking out for me. He said he'd been reading the *Wall Street Journal* that morning and he'd seen an ad for a job opening and that he thought it might be just the thing for me. I asked what the job was and he said he wasn't sure but it sounded like sales. So I asked him who the job was with and he said, "*The Reader's Digest.*"

I don't honestly know if I believed in "signs" back then. I was still pretty young and I had turned my back on my Catholic upbringing. I thought of myself as a pretty hard-nosed, no-bullshit guy who didn't buy into things I couldn't touch, taste, feel, hear, or see. I wasn't having it with fairy tales. So, probably I didn't believe in signs. I imagine I considered it an amusing coincidence that my roommate would call to alert me about a job with the *Readers Digest* when I was spending most of my waking hours lost in back issues of that magazine.

But my life since then has taken me down paths I never would have imagined (mercifully) back then and I believe things now that I wouldn't have believed back then. I have also believed some things—especially when I was in the manic phase of my disease—that make a belief in signs seem like a small, harmless superstition. But we'll come to those later. For now, let me say that I believe life has a way of telling you things, of showing you the way when you are confused or lost and that you should believe in those signs and act on them with conviction. They may be the *only* thing showing you the way and you just have to trust them and trust yourself.

It would have been easy enough to ignore my roommate's tip, to slip back into my thick, lethargic mood and return to reading old magazines. But, when he read off the number from the *Wall Street Journal* ad, I wrote it down. And, later, I made the call.

It turned out that the *Digest* was advertising for someone to fill an opening for a sales position in Washington D.C.. That was convenient since I already had a place to live there, complete with a roommate and with furniture I owned. I'd been eager to get out of Washington but it wouldn't be so bad going back, I thought, if I had a good job with a great company like the *Digest*. According to the ad in the Journal, the interviews would be held in a Manhattan hotel and, for some reason, they would stretch out over a couple of days. I got on the phone and made a reservation. Then I packed went down to New York.

I wasn't sure what to expect. A typical job interview, I imagine. The kind where you fill out a bunch of forms and questionnaires, maybe take a test or two, and then you go into a room and sit across a desk from someone who asks you questions about yourself. You tell him why it has been your dream, for as long as you can remember, to work for his company. Maybe you talk a little bit about salary and benefits and you try not to sound too mercenary. He thanks you for coming and says someone will be in touch. You get up and go home and wait for the phone to ring.

Well, what I got was something completely different.

These were the early days of "human resources" specialists and "industrial psychology," and all sorts of new techniques for dealing with personnel decisions and management. And the *Digest* was a rich company and a forward looking outfit and they were on the cutting edge of these things. So this was no ordinary job interview. It was more like an audition for a part in a play or television series. I believe that the whole thing was built around what they were calling "stress techniques." Which involved putting you on the spot and watching how you handled yourself.

There were 50 or 60 of us who showed up the first morning. All men and most of them around my age. Guys like me who were looking for a career change and were drawn in by the idea of working for a great outfit like the *Digest*.

We did some conventional things. Filled out the usual forms and took the little multiple-choice psychological tests. Then, we got into the innovative stuff. First, each of us had to get up on a stage in this theatre, with the rest of the applicants sitting out in the audience, and demonstrate the ability to sell a product. They gave us different things to sell and I got lucky. They gave me a can of tennis balls and since I'd played in both high-school and college, I was very confident I could make the sale to the "client" who was somebody from the *Digest* personnel department. You made your pitch to him while other people from the *Digest*, out there in the dark, watched and gave you a grade.

My turn came and I went to work, giving everything I had to the selling of a can of tennis balls. The lessons I'd learned from wearing dirty clothes and going around the neighborhood on my bicycle, selling strawberries, must have served me well. My tennis ball pitch was good enough that I made the cut. A dozen or so of us were told to come back the next day for what sounded like the final exam.

This was the "stress interview." You were on stage, again. And there were people out there in the dark, again, watching how you performed. A guy who was supposed to be tough, I suppose, started asking you these aggressive questions and you were supposed to answer them. I think they were looking for how well you stood up to the questions. Could you keep your cool?

I was always cocky in situations like this. I don't know why and I certainly can't say that it was justified at the time. I was out of work and tying to come to some sort of terms with this terrible secret affliction, so I didn't have a lot to be cocky about. Still, that's how I was. Maybe being so recently out of the military had something to do with it. I'd been yelled at and I wasn't going to go to pieces just because some stranger raised his voice at me in a fake job interview.

Well, we were going along. The interviewer would ask a question and I'd answer it. He'd challenge my answer and I'd defend it. I wasn't particularly upset or angry. In fact, I thought the whole thing was kind of funny.

We'd been going back and forth for a while when the interview said to me, "So what's your greatest weakness?"

"I don't know," I said. "I guess I'm lazy."

"Lazy?"

"That's right."

"Well what do you do about it?"

"I fight it."

"*Fight it?*" the interviewer said, with this belligerent edge.

"That's right."

"Well, tell me, how do you fight it? Do you stay in bed every day until eleven O'clock fighting it."

And, at that point, I laughed. Pretty hard, in fact. I couldn't help myself.

"Why are you laughing?" the interviewer said.

"Because that's a funny line."

Just then, a voice from out of the dark said, "Hire him."

And that's how I got the job that changed my life. Because I laughed when somebody asked me a stupid question.

There's a lesson in there somewhere. I'm sure of it.

CHAPTER 6

CHAPTER 6

Being hired by the *Reader's Digest* was a big thing in my life and it was not until much later that I realized how large this event actually loomed and how much it influenced everything that came after. At the time, I was more relieved than anything else. I'd always known that I would get another job and go back to work. What I didn't know was: who I would be working for and where would I be working.

Now I knew.

Of course, the fact that my new employer was the *Reader's Digest* meant a lot. These were the days when people took a job with one of the big, iconic companies—IBM or GM or the *Digest*—with the expectation that they would never leave. Their lives would consist of a steady climb up the corporate ladder, promotion following promotion, until they attained some prosperous senior management position followed by retirement. While I'd been hired by one of those companies, I didn't feel that way. My horizons did not extend that far.

I've thought about the reasons for this and I believe my secret had something to do with it. I was different … even if I could not say so and did not know why. So I did not simply assume that I had found a career and a home and that I would be with the *Digest* forever. Since this thing without a name had taken me by surprise, I had become wary of that kind of thinking. It was a big unknown and it made everything else in my life unknowable.

Still, I threw myself into the work.

I would be responsible for getting the *Digest* into supermarkets, in those racks that you see in every checkout line these days. Back then, the stores had to be sold on the idea of these racks and then somebody had to install them. That would be my job. I did my training, for a couple of months, back in Washington and then I set off for my new territory. Which was Texas—the eastern half of the state—and Louisiana. I would be based in Houston.

It was not a good fit. I'd lived almost all my life in the eastern United States. I felt at home there and I especially loved New England. Houston was a different world. It was hot and big and empty. The people seemed loud and aggressive and hard for me to get to know. I felt alone and out of place.

I found a small apartment. It had an air-conditioner that took forever to cool the place. When I came back to the apartment after being on the road, I would turn the air-conditioner on and then leave for a couple of hours until the place was bearable. The building had a pool but the water was so warm that when you got in, it was like taking a bath. So instead of going swimming while I waited for the apartment to cool down, I would go around the corner to a bar and have a couple of drinks.

I was alone and I was out of place. But I did have my work. So I made my rounds, giving my pitch, and when I made a sale, I would install the racks myself with a tool called a "hog-ringer." This was a long, curved pair of pliers that farmers would use to put a ring in the nose of a hog. It was perfect for installing those racks and I got pretty handy with it. If I'd lost my attaché case, anyone who found it would have been mystified by the contents. Promotional material, contracts, copies of the *Digest*, and this wicked looking tool along with these rings designed to go in the nose of a hog. But those were the tools of my trade. And I was good with them.

One other essential was an automobile. I had a big territory and I covered it by driving those long Texas highways, so the *Digest* bought me a car and since I got to pick it out, it was a beauty.

The car was a '62 Chevy Bel Air convertible. It was painted autumn gold with a red stripe and it had red leather upholstery. I loved that car. It made the long hours on the highway not just bearable but actually kind of pleasant.

But pleasant is not how I would characterize my time in Houston, overall. I was lonely and out of my natural element. But there was one way in which it might have been the right place for me to be.

It was a good place for me to hide out.

As I said earlier—and as I can't stress strongly enough—I was desperate to keep my condition (whatever it was) a secret. I was terrified that it might get out. To have it known that I suffered from some kind of "mental illness" … I couldn't imagine, at that time, anything more stigmatizing and humiliating.

And, in Houston, there was no one who was likely to find out and expose me. I was all alone. No office and no colleagues. My boss was in Washington so I hardly ever saw him. We kept in touch by phone and since I was doing a good job of opening new accounts, there was no need for him to come down and check up on me. So my secret was safe.

But just because nobody knew, that didn't mean that this thing had gone away. I had some bad days—bad weeks, even—when I was in Houston. Some of them very bad. But no one had to know, except for me and a very kind doctor.

His name was Fred Marceau and he was from Louisiana. He began seeing me after I had gone to the hospital in Houston and asked to be treated on an outpatient basis. I paid out of my own pocket, instead of submitting the bills to the insurance company. I didn't want the *Digest* to find out.

Dr. Marceau didn't have any answers for me. He believed, like the man I'd seen in Hawaii, that I was schizophrenic. And there was no drug therapy for people like me in those days. That was still almost a decade away and I didn't begin to take medication for longer than that. So what Dr. Marceau and I did was talk.

But it helped. It was reassuring and comforting and a big part of that was the personality of the person I was talking to. Dr. Marceau had the gift of empathy. It is a rare thing and something I sensed when we talked.

He did not deal with me as a clinician and he did not condescend or patronize me. I don't remember, all these years later, exactly what we talked about but I know that something came through to me in those talks and it helped me at a time when nothing else did.

During the time I was in Houston, I never experienced another attack like the one in Hawaii that had been the first sign that something was badly wrong. I wasn't overcome with that sense of near-panic. What I did struggle with was a sense of what I would call profound anxiety, something that bordered on dread but that didn't have any real cause that I could connect the feeling to.

This is the essence of the bi-polar condition (as I have come to learn) and, indeed, of any psychiatric illness. What you experience emotionally is unconnected to the external realities of your life. We have all had a reason to feel unhappy or depressed but someone who suffers from clinical depression feels that way acutely and worse, for no reason. The normal rules of cause and effect seem suspended and you are out there in a universe where you can't explain why you feel the way you do and there doesn't seem to be any way to go about changing or fixing things. If you don't know what is making you feel depressed or anxious, how can you take steps to make yourself feel better? In an emotional universe where there is no cause and effect ... just these unexplained effects, you are reduced to a kind of helplessness and impotence that makes what you are already feeling that much worse. You have no control and you don't know what is coming next. And this describes, I think, a kind of terror that those of us who suffer from these conditions must come to understand and deal with.

As I say, my symptoms while I was in Houston could probably best be described as acute anxiety. Again, there was no reason for me to feel this kind of pervasive sense of foreboding. I was doing my job. Nobody was out to do me harm. Anyone looking at my life from the outside would have seen a lonely man spending a lot of time on the road, living in a place he didn't like much, and doing well in his work. Someone, in short, who had reason to feel, at worst, a mild sense of discontent with his life. Some restlessness, perhaps, but nothing more serious than that.

What I experienced though, was this intense physical anxiety. I would come over me so strongly that my palms would begin sweating and I would actually begin to tremble. I would begin breathing so rapidly that I felt like I might hyperventilate and I would feel my heart racing like it was almost out of control. And all this might happen when I was doing something as innocuous as sitting at a table in my stuffy little apartment writing up my expense reports.

Back then, I didn't know why I felt this way and that, of course, made it all the worse. There was no name (not one I would use, anyway) for what I was experiencing. Nothing to help me understand it, control it, or prepare myself for what might come next. All this, of course, made things worse.

That was a long time ago and I have been through a lot since then and learned a lot. Some of it by trial and error, some of it through my own research, and some of it from professionals who know so much more now than they did when Dr. Marceau and I would have those talks.

Perhaps the most important of the things I've learned is this: whatever the symptom, it will pass. I cannot stress, strongly enough, to fellow bi-polar patients, this lesson. If you are in pain and think it may never end, that can be—literally—unendurable. But if you know, of a certainty, that the pain will go away, then you can just bear down and endure it until you get to the other side. We've all done that, when the pain is physical.

But when you think that, say, anxiety like the kind I was experiencing in Houston might never go away, that just makes you more anxious. The worse things seem, the worse they get, until you have no reason to believe the cycle will ever end. And hopelessness is, as we all know, unendurable.

But as I say, I now know that whatever the symptoms of my condition, with time they will go away. And this makes them easier to bear even if it does not make them vanish.

Also, I gradually learned that when I was feeling this kind of anxiety, I needed to do some simple things to try to get on top of it. It can help to just stop. By that I mean, you quit doing whatever it is you are doing and you don't try to start doing something else until you have gotten control of your breathing and your pulse and the world around you no longer seems quite so threatening. There are breathing exercises and meditation techniques for this but by the time I had heard about them, I was used to doing things my own way.

The essential thing is to realize what is happening. When you've done this, you can do whatever works best for you to stop the acceleration of this nameless, formless dread.

When I talked with Dr. Marceau, all those years ago, simply telling him what I was feeling and trying to describe what I was going through, actually made me feel better. I learned, gradually, that by recognizing these symptoms and pushing back against them—even if it was by merely sitting down in a chair and getting control over my breathing—that I was doing the same thing that I had done with him. I was no longer simply and passively reacting and letting my condition take control.

It sounds simple. Too simple, in fact. But we all know that in this life, the simplest things can be very hard. When you are in a state of deep depression, relief can come from just *doing* something. But it can be impossibly, insurmountably difficult to make yourself do anything at all. Even something as simple is getting dressed in the morning.

I know. I've been there, too. But that came later. After I'd left Houston.

CHAPTER 7

While the time in Houston was far from the happiest of my life, it was not wasted. Not in the remotest sense of the word. For one thing, I was building a reputation with the *Digest* and that was important for all the obvious reasons. I wanted to make a career for myself; wanted to succeed. And I was doing that, going around and convincing people with the various chains that it would be a good idea to have a rack displaying the *Reader's Digest* and *TV Guide* right up next to the cash register in the check-out lane where people couldn't miss them and couldn't resist. Those two titles had the highest circulation of any magazines in the country and there they would be, in the same rack, right when the customer was reaching into her pocketbook to pay for her groceries. I didn't have to work too hard to convince my clients that those racks were a good idea. And then, when I'd made the sale, I'd send in a report to my boss who saw increased sales and increased revenues and that was good for both of us.

It wasn't my dream job—I didn't even like it much—but I was succeeding at it and that counted for a lot.

And, then, I was learning some techniques for dealing with my illness (though I wasn't calling it that) even if I didn't realize it.

When you are depressed or experiencing anxiety—the way I was when I was in Houston—the temptation is to withdraw. Everything seems so hard or so fraught with some kind of unnamed danger that you just want to hide in your room or stay in bed or do something to avoid having to face the world. And when you are faced with this kind of urge to retreat, the easiest thing is to simply give in to it.

Even though it wasn't always easy, I never did that.

I don't want to sound like I am somehow braver or tougher than other people who suffer from bi-polar illness. I don't believe that. But I do know that even on my worst days, back in Houston, when I didn't feel like I could face the world, I somehow made myself do it. I would go out on the road and make my calls and sell those racks. I would drive around to the supermarkets where I had made those sales and I would install the racks with my hog ringer. And then I would go back to my dismal little apartment and write up my reports. It wasn't always easy but I managed to do it and learning how to do that was what got me through a lot of tough times in the years to come, times before I was able to put a name to my condition and before I began to take the drugs that had become available to treat it. Those were times when all I could do was tough it out. Some of the lessons I learned during my Houston years, when I wasn't even aware I was learning them, helped enormously.

I guess I became so accustomed to my life in Houston and on the road that I didn't realize how other people might have looked at it. To me, it was just what I did every day. But there was this one incident that made me realize that my job wasn't as easy as it looked. Dealing with my condition had already made me tough; I was accustomed to discomfort. It happened when I was on the road with a young man who'd been sent down by the *Digest* to travel around and make calls with me as a way of breaking him into the business. He was a nice young fellow from a wealthy family in Atlanta and he was eager to learn the business and excited by the prospect of a career with the *Digest*.

So after I'd talked with him and told him a little about what we'd be doing, we got in my car and headed for Louisiana where I would be making some calls on the Piggly Wiggly chain.

It was hot. Mid-summer. And we were in the bayou country so it wasn't just hot; it was also damp. You stepped outside and you were immediately soaking wet. There was something oppressive about it. The heat and the humidity just took it out of you. By the end of the day, we were done in.

We had to find a place to spend the night. The *Digest* gave us a generous expense account, certainly enough to stay at the best place in any town where we were likely to be making calls. But there was only one motel in this town and it was pretty much of a dump. And to make things worse, there was only one vacancy. We couldn't even have separate rooms.

The good news, I suppose, is that there were two beds in the room.

So we found a place to eat, though in that heat, it was pretty hard to work up much of an appetite. Then we went back to that little motel and the room we were sharing for the night.

I think my young trainee was already starting to feel a twinge of disillusionment. This wasn't the life he had in mind when he was hired by the *Digest*.

I don't remember if there was a television in our little motel room but if there was, I suppose we watched some television. I do remember that the motel was built out next to one of those bayous or canals that you see all over southern Louisiana and that are just perfect for breeding mosquitoes. They were swarming and we had to kill a number that got into our room when we opened the door.

So we closed everything up tight and turned the air-conditioner up full blast. It was an old unit that didn't fit properly in the window. It was held in place by a couple of sheets of plywood that had been nailed to the window frame. The air-conditioner vibrated and made a hell of a racket when the condenser kicked in. It was a long time before I got to sleep and I don't know if the trainee ever did.

For me, it was just another day on the road. For him … well, it was something else, entirely. And it got worse.

In the middle of the night, I woke up when the air-conditioner started vibrating so badly that it was impossible to sleep.

"What should we do?" the trainee said.

"I don't know," I told him. "But if we turn it off, we'll roast in here."

"I guess you're right."

Eventually, the condenser shut down and the room was quiet enough that I could go back to sleep. But that didn't last long. The condenser kicked in again and the air conditioner started vibrating and while I was lying there looking at it, it just shook itself right out of that improvised, plywood mount, fell out of the window, and went into the bayou with a splash.

I lay there in bed, looking at this big hole where the air conditioner had been and where the mosquitoes were now pouring into our room.

That one trip to Louisiana was enough to convince the trainee that he'd make the wrong career choice. He went back to Atlanta and found a job in the family business.

I stayed, of course, and there were long days when things didn't go right and days when, even if things did go right, I felt like I was doing work that anyone could do. Days when, in other words, I felt like I wasn't really getting anywhere and wasn't really making the most of whatever gifts and talents I had. The same feelings we all have, at one time or another, about our work, careers, and lives.

These doubts and questions and frustrations didn't have anything to do with my condition but I learned something about myself from dealing with them.

Namely, that I could put up with these feelings and keep going. It is a lesson we all have to learn. We put up with frustrations of the present; deal with them the best we can and even conquer them, in the hope that things will get better or turn around in the future. The best way, it seems, to help that better future along is to do the best you can with the present.

So you sell another supermarket manager on the idea of magazine rack at the checkout counter and then you go in and install it with a hog-ringer.

And, one day, you get a call from the *Digest*. The home office wants to talk to you about a program they've developed for helping kids who are slow readers. Your boss wants you to go around to the schools in your territory and sell them on this program. It won't cost them much and it has a great potential for helping kids who need it.

Well, it wasn't something I knew much about. But it was something new and I was ready for that, since racking stories was getting just a little old. It was also a challenge and I was ready for that, too. So I studied the product thoroughly because I wanted to understand exactly what I was selling. I wanted to believe in it and once I'd made myself familiar with it, I did.

The program was simplicity, itself. I consisted of a series of books for all the lower school grades. The thing was, some of the books were more advanced and difficult than others but you couldn't tell that from looking at the cover. The content of the books had been carefully researched and developed—in those days, the *Digest* was very prosperous and never cut corners or did things on the cheap. The material was geared to the ability of each grade and then to a subset of each grade—advanced readers, the average readers, the slow reader … and so on. The books cost about ten cents each and each kid got a new one at the beginning of every month of the school year. So the cost was less than a dollar a kid.

All these years later, when I tell someone about that program and how well it was designed, I find myself getting excited. And—well, I can't help myself—I start *selling* it, just like I did back when I was calling on schools in little rural towns all over Texas and Louisiana.

Of course, in those days, in that part of the country, there were two schools in every little town—one white and one black—and I would call on both of them. I'd usually get a polite but cool reception at the white school. Not exactly a brush-off, but pretty close. They had plenty of money and they had lots of resources. They didn't really need a new program. But they would listen to my pitch and look at my samples. Mostly, I think, because I was from the *Digest* and it was such a powerful brand back then.

So I made a fair number of sales in the white schools. I had become a good salesman, after all. But I was a long way from batting one thousand.

The people at the black schools, on the other hand, were delighted to see me. I mean, really enthusiastic. They treated me like I was doing them a favor, instead of the other way around. They listened to my pitch and they looked at the material I brought with me and they asked questions. Then, they almost always signed up for the program and thanked me on my way out.

I made follow-up calls at those schools and the people were glad to see me and eager to tell me about how happy they were with the program and what good results they were seeing from it.

Their gratitude was sincere and there was something very touching about it. I know, for one thing, that part of it came from the fact that they hardly ever saw any white faces and when they did, it was usually not someone coming with good news or a way to help them out.

I also think—and this may be a stretch—that the people I dealt with in those schools sensed that I was an outsider in that part of the world and because of that, they were sympathetic. I had grown up mostly in the northeast and I hadn't had much contact with black people or with hostility to them. At first, I didn't approach the people in those black schools as anything other than potential clients. I was a salesman trying to close a deal. But I felt a kind of connection with them almost right away.

Nothing I experienced in Texas, in the way of alienation, was a patch on what those people went through every day but I still think, just the same, that there was some mutual empathy. We connected, in some way, that went beyond my selling a product and their buying it. When I went back on those follow-ups, people were glad to see me and it showed. And I was genuinely glad to see them and I think that showed, too.

The reading program was a big success. With the schools and the students and, also, with the *Digest*. And when it came to selling the program, I had the best numbers in the company. People wrote to thank me and they wrote the *Digest* and somehow the state of Texas got in on all the praise for me and the program and I was made an "honorary Texan" and honored in a special ceremony. There was a plaque and it was presented to me by John Connally who was governor of the state at the time and would be riding in the car with John Kennedy, a few months later, when they were both shot. Kennedy, of course, fatally.

Even though I didn't like the place much, I was proud to be made an honorary Texan and I still have that plaque. But it meant more to me to be a success selling the program and having the *Digest* recognize it. My bosses back at headquarters were good, after all, for a lot more than a plaque and a few "attaboys." But I think that what meant more to me than either of those things was the way I was received and treated by the people in those black schools.

I was trying to keep a very big secret in my life. I was afraid that the world would somehow find out and consider my secret shameful and that I would be treated that way. That the world would see me as a freak. So I felt *different*, in a very difficult way.

A way that was almost oppressive. When you are keeping a secret, you feel like you can't possibly be intimate—or even very friendly, with other people. So you stay on guard and you keep people at arm's length and that's just the way it is.

But the people in those black schools were so trusting and accepting of me. And so genuinely grateful that I showed an interest in them and their problems …

We didn't become friends outside of our business relationships, of course, or anything close to it. I saw them in those schools and nowhere else. But they treated me in a way that made it possible for me to feel normal human impulses of generosity and trust and gratitude. It's something I'll never forget.

Texas was a lonely, anxious time for me but my sessions with Dr. Marceau and my dealings with the people in those schools kept me in touch with the rest of the human race and with the ordinary kindnesses. In those moments, I didn't feel like my condition had somehow exiled me from the world of other people.

That made a lot of difference back then.

And still does, now.

CHAPTER 8

CHAPTER 8

One day, I decided that I'd had enough. Just like that. Enough of Houston. Enough of the heat. Enough of yet another lonely drive down a long empty highway to one more little town for still another call on another supermarket. Enough of hog-ringing magazine racks.

So I called the *Digest* and said I wanted to speak to Jim Kreider. He was the man in charge of personnel. The operator asked me for my name and then said, "Please hold a moment."

"Steve," Jim said, warmly. "Good to hear from you. How are you doing?"

He was a very nice guy and we'd always been friendly.

"I'm fine, Jim," I said. "Listen, I'm calling because I want to know if you folks up in Pleasantville think I'm doing a good job down here."

"Doing a good job? Well, *of course* we think you're doing a good job. The numbers are great. And the work you did on the reading program was outstanding. Best in the company. By a long way. You're doing a great job, Steve. Why?"

"Well," I said. "I'm glad to hear you think I'm doing such a great job. Because I quit."

When I said that, there was this silence from the other end. Like the phone had gone dead.

"Quit? Why do you want to *quit*? I just said you are doing a great job."

"Jim," I said, "I've had all I can take of saddles and horses and cowboy hats. I'm not a Texan. I come from the East. And I've had enough of racking grocery stores, and selling schoolbooks. That's not a *career*. I want you to bring me back to Pleasantville where I can do something with a future."

"Well, then" Jim said, very quickly, before I could get another word in, "if that's it, we can work something out. Don't quit. Give me some time. We'll find something for you even if it isn't in Pleasantville right away."

"Okay, Jim," I said. "Thanks. I'll be waiting for your call."

When I hung up the phone, it occurred to me that Kreider could just as easily have said, "Okay, then, go ahead and quit, Hotshot. We'll send someone down to replace you. And don't forget to hand over the keys to that car we bought for you."

But he hadn't said that. If I'd been bluffing, then my bluff had worked. But I hadn't been bluffing. I meant every word even though I didn't have another job lined up and wasn't all that sure I could find one. But everything I'd said to Jim was true. I was tired of Texas and fed up with racking supermarkets and selling on the road and if that was my future then I was ready to quit.

Now, I'm sure it has occurred to some readers—just as it has occurred to me— to ask this question: "Why did you want to leave Texas when you've said that being there allowed you to hide out and keep your secret? Weren't you afraid that, if you were brought back to the main office in Pleasantville, the secret would get out? That you would be exposed, stigmatized, and ruined?"

And my answer is … "No. I wasn't thinking that way. Not during the time I made my decision and especially not on the day I made that call."

I didn't know then what I know now. About myself and my condition. But here is what I now believe was going on back then:

Bi-polar illness is unpredictable in every way. It comes and it goes and sometimes it manifests itself one way and on other occasions, in a different—

even opposite—way. Some days you are depressed or anxious and some days you are up. Even gloriously up. Dangerously, exuberantly up, in ways that I would soon experience and that would nearly ruin me. And then ... some days, you are just another normal human, reacting normally to the world around you and your own circumstances.

It is a crap shoot. One morning, you wake up and you are in the barrel. Or, you could be on the mountaintop—king of the world. And then, there are days when you are just old Steve Millard, down in Texas, working hard and doing a good job and itching to get ahead in the world.

I now understand that when I made that call to Jim Kreider, threatening to quit, that I was probably in a period when I was at the baseline. I was neither up nor down. My emotional state was "normal" and by that, I mean I was responding to events and situations in the way you would expect someone to. It was perfectly predictable that I'd be feeling both cocky and frustrated. I was doing a good job—a damned good job—for the *Digest* and I knew it. And I was justifiably resentful because I felt like the people back at headquarters didn't appreciate the good job I was doing and that they were perfectly prepared to leave me out Texas, where I felt exiled and where I would never be able to move up and take on more responsibility and have the kind of successful career I felt was my destiny.

So I was ready to quit. I wasn't thinking about hiding out and keeping secrets because the disease was sleeping and I was just a normal young man with normal desires and emotions. I wanted to get ahead and I wanted to be in on the action.

One of the things I've learned in more than 40 years of dealing with my bi-polar illness—and that I've made a rule in my life—is that you should *never* make an important, potentially life-changing decision when you are depressed or anxious. You'll make the wrong call ... if not every time, then most of the time.

You see, it isn't *you* doing the thinking when this happens. The disease is in control and with whatever little bit of clarity you have left, you need to recognize this and make sure you don't give in to what amounts to an impulse and not a rational thought. You can do tremendous damage to yourself if you act on these impulses. You can even take it to the ultimate and destroy yourself … literally. Like the 15 to 20 percent of bi-polar sufferers who commit suicide.

I was there, almost, myself. That night by the pond. With the Lugar.

But saying that you should fight and resist those impulses—usually self-destructive—that come over you when you are depressed or anxious, is *not* to say that you should just turn into a cautious, timid person who never takes any risks. When you are not feeling anxious or depressed, when the disease is hibernating or in remission or whatever you want to call it … that's when you should trust your instincts and if you are considering some bold stroke … well then go for it. I always did that. And I am so grateful that I did. Otherwise, I might still be out on the road, somewhere, calling on supermarkets.

But I *knew* that I needed a change. And I was the only one who knew and the only one who could do something about it. So I made it happen.

And calling Jim Kreider and threatening to quit is just one example. Later in my career, but still before I had been formally diagnosed as bi-polar and begun drug therapy, I made the decision to go out on my own and start a business. When I made that decision, I had one client and just enough money to last six months.

It was the biggest gamble of my life and I made it knowing that it might trigger some of the worst possible consequences—both financial and psychological. I could very easily go broke at an age when making a comeback from financial ruin would be hard, if not impossible. And that wasn't the worst of the possibilities. The stress of the change might, I knew, trigger an attack of some sort. I might fall off into a severe depression and who could say what that might lead to? Or, it might go the other way, into mania. This was the most frightening possibility of all ... but that is getting way ahead of the story.

The point is, I made my decision—a life changing decision—at a time when I was "normal." My emotions were base line and I was not in the grip of impulses that had nothing to do with my real-world situation. And it turned out to be the right decision. Very, very much so.

I became an entrepreneur, built a business along with a name and a reputation, and I made enough money to become financially secure and do all the things I wanted to do. I did it in spite of the fact that I was bi-polar and had not yet gone into treatment of any kind. Because, by then, I had learned a lot about my condition, even if it didn't know it by name and wasn't taking any kind of drugs to control it. But I knew some things—had learned them the hardest way, by experience. I knew when I should—and shouldn't—make that kind of big decision.

One final thing, before we return to my story—to the *Digest* and what happened after Texas: Readers may ask, "Well, if you shouldn't make big decisions when you are depressed or anxious—when you are in the "down" phase of the emotional curve—what about when you are manic or "up?"

If you have been there—as I have—you will know the answer to that question. When you are manic, you do not "make choices." They are made for you even though you feel like you are making them and you are absolutely convinced that everything you do is not just right, but inspired and brilliant. You are infallible. Bullet proof. Everything but immortal and maybe even that, too. It is a wild, terrifying ride.

But we'll come to that a little further along in the story.

CHAPTER 9

CHAPTER 9

J im Kreider was as good as his word. He got me out of Houston. But he couldn't get me transferred to headquarters. Not immediately, anyway. But he did get me back east, to a place that felt more like home. Pittsburgh.

It was a good move … and a bad move. Good, because it got me out of Texas where I'd always felt like an outsider. Bad, because even though the location had changed, my job hadn't. I was still racking supermarkets.

But the change of venue was enough, at first, and I threw myself into my work and got to know my new environment. I remember particularly a little bar where I would go after a hard day. I'd have a drink or two and listen to this blind piano player who was really very good and got to be kind of a friend. Somehow he would know when I arrived, even if I hadn't spoken a word. He would smile and play one of my favorite songs.

But though the move was good for me, it didn't mean I had left all my troubles behind me, in Texas. There were still those days when I would feel anxious or depressed for no good reason. Unusually and extremely depressed or anxious so that I knew something was seriously wrong with me; that this infirmity that had first surfaced in Hawaii was still with me. That it had followed me back to the states. First to Washington, then to Texas, and now to Pittsburgh. I knew, I suppose, that I wasn't going to shed it by changing my address or my job. That it would be with me, perhaps, all my life. But I didn't know what to do about it and nobody else did, either. Not even the kindly Dr. Marceau, who I had left behind when I moved from Texas to Pittsburgh.

There was one occasion, I remember, when things got so bad that I called a hospital, looking for the same kind of help I'd found in Houston, as a psychiatric outpatient. But nothing came of it. I never saw anyone. I was completely on my own.

So I kept doing what I'd been doing to keep going and stay on top of things. Doing, I suppose, what had worked, off and on, in the past. I relied on denial and bluff and the little strategies that I'd developed without actually realizing I was doing it. When I was feeling at my worst, that's when I would try hardest to make myself just *do* something. Whatever that needed to be done, even if it wasn't really important or urgent, just something small and routine like straightening my apartment or washing my car. I tried to stay busy. It seemed to help though I couldn't say why.

And, of course, I had my work. And even though I'd lost any real enthusiasm for it, I kept pounding the pavement, selling supermarkets on the idea of putting those magazine racks in the checkout line. And I made sales. Lots of sales. So the *Digest* had every reason to be happy with my work even if I didn't.

Then, after several months of it, on a day when I was feeling strong and confident, I picked up the phone and called Jim Kreider in Pleasantville.

"Jim," I said, "it's Steve. I hadn't heard anything and I just wanted to call and make sure that you people were happy with the work I'm doing here in Pittsburgh."

"Absolutely, Steve," Kreider said. "You're doing great."

"Good," I said, "because I quit."

And I meant it. Just like I had when we'd gone through this before. I was done racking stores.

"No, Steve. Please, don't do that. I've been working on getting you something here. Give me a few more days."

So I agreed and, again, Jim came through for me. When he called me back it was to tell me that there might be an opening in the book and records division of the company, working for a man named Frank Ronnenberg.

Jim said that this Ronnenberg would come talk to me at a meeting I would be attending in Florida. It was an annual thing where the team of guys who did what I did—who went around racking stores—would get together someplace nice for a few days. We'd exchange ideas and play golf. Eat and drink … mostly drink. It was kind of a morale boosting deal for those of us who were out there working our territories. There were only about a dozen of us—we had big territories—and we all liked one another and felt this kind of camaraderie. In our minds, it was as though we were part of some kind of special breed in the *Digest* scheme of things. And, in a way, we were. We were the lone operators, getting the job done alone and without a lot of support or supervision. And now this guy from headquarters would be coming to our meeting to look for someone to bring in from the field and put to work on his staff.

It would be a big chance for at least one of us. And I wanted that person to be me. Wanted it badly. But I wasn't nervous or afraid.

Frank Ronnenberg would become one of the most important people in my life and a man to whom I owe a huge, unpayable debt. But when I first met him, at the conference in Florida, I thought he was kind of gruff and humorless and something of a tough guy. I was wrong about the first part—he had a terrific sense of humor—and half right about the second part. Frank was a no-nonsense business guy who believed in getting the job done and if he had to ride people to do it, then he'd ride them. He was in charge of one of the big moneymaking operations at the *Digest* and he kept the pressure on people to make sure it stayed that way. Of course, there was nothing unusual about that in corporate America in those days.

But Frank was also a good family man—he had a wife and five kids he was devoted to and he was one of those leaders who looked out for his people. He would give you a chance to try something out and he'd back you up on it. And he'd praise you if it worked out. He wasn't one of these bureaucratic sharpshooters who take all the credit and pass all the blame. People who worked for Frank were loyal because he inspired loyalty.

I knew none of this, of course, when he interviewed me at the resort, outside of Jacksonville, Florida. I just saw this big, stern, gruff guy from the home office who wanted to interview me to see if he wanted me to come to work for him. I wanted to come to work for him … well, actually, that wasn't the case. I wanted to get to Pleasantville and start learning something and setting myself up for a career in the business world instead of spending my time on the road and in supermarkets. Frank was my entry so I tried hard to impress him in that interview. I figured I could learn to work for him even if his temperament seemed a little forbidding.

As we've seen, I tend to do well in job interviews but I couldn't get any sense of how I was doing with Frank. I left the interview without being sure either way.

But a little later—it couldn't have been more than a few days—I got a call and learned I had the job.

I was happy. Of course, I was happy. It was what I wanted. It got me out of a life that had become stale, routine, and boring. One with no future. I was more than happy. I was thrilled.

And I was also a little apprehensive but, actually, not as apprehensive as I should have been. Here's why:

I knew I had this nameless condition. Nameless, because I couldn't stand to use the one label that I'd ever heard put on it—*schizophrenia*. And I knew that it hadn't gone away even though I was in what I later came to think of as a "normal" or "baseline" state. I knew that it was more than likely—and probably certain—that I'd suffer from more attacks of either depression or anxiety and that I'd have to go out and bluff my way through it, the way I'd been doing when I was on my own in Houston and Pittsburgh. Only now, I'd be in Pleasantville, in an office with other people, and nowhere to hide.

And, then, there was something else that I was a long way from being able to put a name to but that I was beginning to suspect in an intuitive sort of way. Something brought my "attacks" on. Much later, I would understand the concept of "triggers" and learn to spot them and deal with them. For now, I just had this vague sense that there were certain things that stimulated attacks and that I ought to do my best to avoid them. And I kind of suspected, all that time ago, that a sudden change of location and scenery might be a "trigger." Not always, but in certain circumstances.

My suspicion from those days has been confirmed many times since then and we'll get to that. But for now, let's just say I was happy—exceedingly happy—to be offered a place in Frank Ronnenberg's shop at the headquarters of the *Reader's Digest* in Pleasantville. I felt some qualms. But they were minor. I was still young. Strong. Confident. And this was what I wanted. So even though I learned later that a big move or change of scenery could act as a trigger and bring on an attack ... it didn't happen this time. I was just too damned happy.

And I kept on feeling happy when I arrived in Pleasantville. First, I went through all the usual stuff with the personnel department and then I met the people I would be working with and I got the tour of the building including the dining room that was catered by Stouffers.

And then they showed me my office.

My own office.

For someone who had been working out of a car or an apartment or a little motel room for what seemed like a lifetime, the idea of an office, all my own, was almost too much. And it wasn't a cubbyhole, either, though I probably wouldn't have minded. It was a proper office, certainly big enough, and it had a window with a view of the beautifully landscaped grounds and the ivy-covered walls of the *Digest* building. And, then, on top of everything, they had someone come around and ask me how I'd like my office decorated.

"Huh," I think I said.

"What color would you like us to paint the walls?"

It took me a minute. Then I told them. "Blue and green."

And that's what I got.

It is difficult to convey, all these years later, what I felt during my first few days at the *Digest*. Having my own office ... that may not seem like such a big deal. It was just an office, after all. People all over the world sat in offices every day and some of those offices were a hell of a lot grander than mine. But that office was a lot more than a workspace to me. It represented something I had wanted this for a long time and now I had it. I was part of the 'A' team; I worked for the *Reader's Digest*, one of America's blue chip companies and I was at headquarters. The company had enough confidence in me to bring me in from the road and put me in my own office. Somehow that validated the confidence that I'd always felt in myself but that I'd doubted from time to time, especially in the dark moments when I was in the grip of this thing I didn't understand or just feeling alone out in the world. Not many of us truly like to feel alone, even if we say we do. And when you suffer from a mental disease—as I did (and do), though I was still in some sort of state of denial back then ... when you suffer from a mental disease, then you feel truly and frighteningly alone. Then you *really* want to belong. To feel like everyone else. To be normal.

For most people, when they are not alone, it means they are either at work or with their family. I did not have a family and up to now, my work had been fairly solitary. I went out on the road by myself. Talked to clients. Ate dinner alone. Then spent the night alone in a motel. When I went home, it was to an apartment where I lived alone. That was work.

Now, all that had changed. I was in this wonderful building, with my own office, working with other people. It wasn't just that my job had changed. My *life* had changed. It was overwhelming. Remembering those first few days, I can still feel some of the excitement that I felt so overwhelmingly back then at having my own office and being asked, "What color do you want it painted."

Every life has its moments and that is one of mine.

CHAPTER 10

CHAPTER 10

As happy as I was to be in Pleasantville (and the name, in my case, seemed to fit), I felt one, small qualm. Namely, I had no idea just what I would be *doing*. I knew only that I would be working for Frank, who had an office right across the hall from mine and that the job would have something to do with books. Frank was in charge of the entire book-publishing arm of the *Digest*. That was his domain and I was now a part of it.

The *Digest*, in those days, was one of the leaders in the field of direct marketing. Which meant, essentially, promoting and selling through the mail. Later, with 800 telephone numbers and credit cards and the computer, direct marketing exploded and became a huge part of the American consumer economy. It made a lot of people very rich and a lot more people comfortably rich and I was one of them. But that is getting ahead of the story.

When I arrived in Pleasantville, in the early 60's, direct marketing still meant promoting and selling through the good old U.S. mail. And the *Reader's Digest* was, along with *Time Life* and *Prentice Hall*, one of the giants in the field. Frank Ronnenberg ruled the book side of the *Digest's* direct mail business.

Frank told me what to do and taught me how to do it. He was my mentor and it is hard to imagine how he could have been a better one. But, then, I was a good student if I do say so, myself. What I lacked in brains, I made up for in initiative and enthusiasm. I was so glad for the opportunity and so fascinated by the operation that I really couldn't get enough. Right from the start, I was always popping into Frank's office with questions and ideas and he was very patient with me. He'd answer my question or tell me why my idea wouldn't work and do it in a way that made me want to work just that much harder though I have to say, in the first flush of things, I don't believe I even thought of what I was doing as "work."

I was just that caught up in all of it.

The machinery of the operation fascinated me. The *Digest*—the little perfect-bound magazine that was such a part of middle-American life back then—had more than 20 million subscribers. They sold a lot of those magazines out of those racks I'd been putting in supermarkets but they sold a whole lot more to people who signed up to get it in the mail for a year or two.

Once someone subscribed, we obviously had a mailing address where we could send promotions for, say, books or records. Postage wasn't terribly expensive, so the cost of sending a promotion to everyone who subscribed to the *Digest* wasn't that much. And it was worth it if you got a big enough response. That part of the operation came down to deciding what products would provoke the strongest response from the people you mailed to and pricing the product correctly. When you got that right, you were in the money.

And that is merely the basic model. You could embellish it on either side. You could add more names and you could give people more reasons—besides product and price—to respond. Adding more names was easy and crude. We would go to R.R. Donnelly, the giant printing company, and buy the names they printed in telephone books. At one time, I think we built our master list up to 80 million names. *Eighty million.*

Now, you don't send out a mailing offering *anything* to 80 million people, unless it is free money. And, even then, your response rate might not be enough to cover your costs. Lots of people would throw the envelope in the mail without opening it and you'd be out the postage on that package.

So, you tried to devise ways to get that mailing list honed down to people who would be likely to open an attractively designed envelope and respond, and you tried to segment your master list into smaller lists that you knew worked for specific kinds of products. The idea was to look for a higher and higher response rate the more you honed the list. A lot of guesswork and intuition went into it back in those days and we were always sitting around and talking about ideas for making this or that list more effective and trying to come up with a new product that we thought would be just right to offer the people on some specific list.

There were teasers that we used to keep people from just throwing those envelopes in the trash. The most effective, and famous, of these was the sweepstakes. Or what we called, around the office, the "sweeps."

Here is how that worked. We'd send out a huge mailing that would say, simply, that you were eligible to be entered in a drawing for so many millions of dollars in prizes. No strings attached. Send back the card and you are entered and your name might be drawn and you'll be a winner. Like the lottery today, only you didn't have to buy anything. Nothing at all.

But when we sent out the "invitation" to join the sweepstakes, we would include a "bonus offer." The pitch would be something along the lines of, "and as long as you are at it, why don't you take us up on this special deal on the *Readers' Digest Almanac?*" Or some other book with the potential for wide sales. The book offer didn't do anything to improve your chances in the sweepstakes drawing and we made that clear in the language of the letter. It was just an add-on. Something we piggy-backed on the mailing. But … the people who got the mailing had a kind of subliminal suspicion that their chances of winning the sweeps would be much better if they also ordered the book.

We did test after test and it always worked out that if we sent out the book offer, by itself, then we'd get a certain percentage of returns. But if we married it to a sweepstakes offer, then the percentage went up by 25%. The only way to account for that was this innate suspicion that by ordering the book, you put yourself in better shape to win, say, a million dollars. You could enter the sweeps for nothing. But, psychologically, you were sure that we'd be mad at you for not ordering the book and that would ruin your chances at the big money.

That's the way people are. And a lot about the whole direct mail industry comes down, simply, to understanding how people work. There is a lot more analytical precision in it these days, including mathematical models that I don't entirely understand, but it still comes down to understanding people and how they work and what little incentives and teasers they will respond to.

That's a lot of what went into those *Digest* sweeps and a lot of what I spent my time thinking about. Especially after Frank put me in charge of the sweeps. It was a big responsibility and I took it seriously. I also loved it.

The *Readers' Digest* sweeps always came at the first of the year. The Post Office guaranteed delivery for January 2nd and we started printing in *July* because of the enormous volume, the millions of pieces that we'd be sending. At first, my work on the sweeps came with the title "promotion coordinator" and that meant that I had to get everyone in the building who was involved in the sweeps singing off the same sheet of music. So I became a kind of internal salesman. I had to convince the requisite people from the different divisions to do things the way Frank and I wanted them done and make sure they got done in time.

I learned a lot about negotiating when I was doing that job. I'd go to someone and say I needed something done by such and such a date, and he would say, "No way in hell we can get it done by then," and I'd start to sweet talk or threaten or compromise, depending on the issue or the person I was dealing with. I learned a lot about people, doing that job, and I also learned a very important lesson that stayed with me from then on. I leaned never to lie.

At first, I used to lie a lot for what I thought were all the right reasons. I'd tell people something that wasn't true so they would do what I knew had to be done. And for a while, it worked. Then, one day, I went to the guy who was in charge of writing the computer-produced letters that went out with the sweeps invitations and did all the little touches that made them look like personal letters that were going out just to *you*. His name was John Aslan and he was a close friend and I looked him in the eye and lied to him. Told him I had to have the letter by, say, July 10th. It wasn't true but I figured that by lying, I'd be sure to get the letter before I really needed it and that I could use the cushion.

Well, my friend found out that I didn't really need the letter until the 20th or whatever it was. He'd been busting his people's asses when he didn't really need to and putting off other jobs that really were more urgent so that he could do mine. Well, he confronted me about it and I actually started to cry. Not from fear, but from guilt and because I was afraid I'd lose a friend. I just looked him in the eye and said, "John, I'm sorry. I'll never do that again."

And I didn't. When you start lying to people, you forget who you've lied to and what the lies are and sooner or later, you get caught.

It was a good lesson. And it helped me a lot, years later, when what I was selling was integrity … to clients who didn't think there was much of it in my particular profession.

So, that was my life at the *Digest*. And to a very large degree, the *Digest* was my life. Like I say, I was fascinated—consumed, even—by my work and by the challenge of using the tools we had and what we knew—or thought we knew—about human nature. We were always refining our mailing lists, breaking them down into segments according to how likely people were to respond to a mailing. We'd have one list that was made up of what we thought of as people who would buy *anything*. These were people who were subscribers to the *Digest* and who belonged to the book club and the record club and who had bought from us before. And we would fight with the record division over who got to use this list first, and how often, because you didn't want to go to the well too often. Frank, by the way, would win those fights because he was tougher than the guy who ran the record division. So that just raised the sense of *esprit* among those of us who were Frank's guys. So we worked harder and tried to come up with new ideas to take advantage of our status and the fact that we had first claim on the best lists.

We would come up with ideas for books and then we'd get an artist to come up with a cover and a writer to do a first chapter and a table of contents and we'd send out an offer for that book. If we got a big enough return, we'd go ahead and commission the writer to finish the book. If not, we'd send the people who did order an apology, a free copy of some book that we had overprinted—like the almanac—and we'd move on to the next thing. And there was always a next thing.

Even now, more than 40 years later, I can feel some of the excitement that I felt, so much more intensely, back in those days. We are all familiar with the stereotypes about corporate life and how it is supposed to be monotonous, stifling, and deadly for the soul. And I suppose those things may be true for some people under some circumstances or even many people under most circumstances. But it wasn't true for me. Certainly not at the *Digest*. Those were the best years of my life. The *Digest* wasn't just a job to me. It was a home. And when I lost that home—which I'll get to soon—it was a very, very big deal. It was, in fact, almost fatal.

But that was later. Before the crash, there were the good times. I loved the work and I liked the people I was working with. We had a Friday night drinking club and we would sit around talking about the job and telling stories. Frank would come by but he couldn't stay long because he had all those kids at home. Everybody else would stick around, for a while, after he left because we all liked each other and there was this sense of camaraderie among us.

But as much as I liked my work, my life was not *all* work.

CHAPTER 11

CHAPTER 11

As happy as I was with my work, my life outside the office was going just that well. I was making good money so, after I'd been in Pleasantville for a while, I bought a house. It was a very nice little two-bedroom place right in the heart of Chappaqua, which was actually the home of the *Digest*. Pleasantville was the next town over but the name was so much more appealing and so much more consistent with the image of the *Digest* that the company made some kind of deal with the Post Office to have the mail delivered and sent and postmarked from there. Pleasantville was synonymous with *Readers' Digest* to millions and millions of people who never knew otherwise.

So I was now a homeowner in one of the nicest little communities in the exurbs of the greatest city in the world. I had a car I loved, an autumn-gold 62 Chevy Impala. I had enough money that I got into the market and made a couple of good picks. This made it possible for me to afford a membership in the Whippoorwill Country Club where I played a lot of tennis and some golf on the weekends.

I also got back to doing something that I had left behind, necessarily, when I left New England and was living in places like Hawaii, Washington, Houston, and Pittsburgh. I took up fly-fishing again.

Fishing had been something I loved since I was a kid and when I say I "loved" it, that's no exaggeration. There are people for whom fishing is some kind of deep, almost spiritual calling. The loveliness of the surroundings, the soothing and ceaseless flow of the water, the beauty of the fish … these things all combine to make the fishing experience something profoundly appealing to people like me.

I had started fishing, on my own, as a kid. I did what kids do. I dug worms and I used whatever tackle I could find or buy or that someone would give me and I went to ponds and lakes and reservoirs and I fished. Later, my grandfather who was a serious sportsman took me under his wing and I would go with him. Still using my old spinning tackle and fishing with worms.

Then, one year, he took me on a trip to the Adirondacks, to a pond he knew and that he had actually stocked, himself, with trout. He put small fish—fry, they are called—into those old-fashioned milk cans and took them back into the pond on a wagon. He dumped the fish in the pond and they grew and spawned and pretty soon, there was a nice population of large, healthy trout in that pond.

So, when my grandfather invited me to go with him, I jumped at the chance. We went back in there by wagon and set up a camp on a bank overlooking the pond. We camped there for the entire month of July and fished out of a canoe that he'd left hidden in the woods. One day, we were out on the pond in that canoe when a hatch of mayflies started coming off the water. They were white and looked a little like moths. My grandfather, who was a fly fisherman, had a fly that was meant to match that mayfly. He called it a "white miller," and he tied one on and started casting to the trout that were rising all around us and taking the real mayflies off the water.

I put a worm on my hook and was getting ready to heave it out into the water when my grandfather said, "No, it's time you learned to fly fish." And he gave me his rod and showed me how to cast and pretty soon I caught my first trout on a fly. I never went back to worms. I was a fly fisherman from then on and a passionate one.

But there weren't any trout streams in Houston and I never cared about bass. Anyway, it always seemed so hot in Texas that I couldn't have imagined going outside to fish or do anything else, for that matter, unless I absolutely had to do it.

Back East, it was different. I was now living just a couple of hours—less, maybe—from the legendary Catskill trout streams like the Beaverkill and the Willowemoc. And I had become reacquainted with my old college friend and fishing partner, Alan Yassky, who lived with his wife and family in Nyack, a dumpy little town (back then) on the other side of the river. Alan sold real estate and he was happy to get away, when he could, and go with me to the Catskills for a weekend of fishing.

There was so much good happening in my life during those years at the *Digest* that I didn't think about either the future or the past. I was absorbed in the present. When I did think about my illness, I began honestly to believe I had left it behind. And that made it possible for me *not* to think about it. And the less I thought about it, the less it meant to me and the less bearing it had on my present, happy life.

This is something I have thought about a lot and thought about seriously and deeply. Why was I able—why am I *still* able—to get on with my life and live it as though I am just like everyone else when I know, rationally, that I am not? According to studies of people who have my condition, about half live as I do. For the other half, life is a matter of being fearful and on guard.

Which is better? I can't speak for everyone but I know that I am grateful—that I literally thank God, every day—for my ability to function as though there were nothing for me to fear. I consider that a gift and one of the greatest of my life.

It is settled medical fact that this condition does not go away—not ever—so I know that there will be *those* days. Those weeks. Even those months. But on the other kind of days, when I am just like everyone else, I don't dwell on the inevitability of those bad days. And why should I?

I like to think that I have trained myself, in many ways, to deal with my illness. I've had doctors who know me well tell me that I have done a good job of it. But this big thing—the ability to function without a sense of dread for what I know will return—that's not something I can take any credit for. Instead, I merely give thanks.

So ... feeling this way and living my life as though I was just like everybody else, led me to think that I was on a path that wouldn't change much for the rest of my life. I was at the *Digest*. I loved it and I was doing well. So I had no thoughts of leaving and just assumed that I would have a job there until I retired. I wasn't consumed by ambition. Didn't want to run the whole company, or anything like that. I expected to be promoted and rise through the ranks and I suppose I thought, occasionally, that I might like to take over for Frank Ronnenberg when he retired one day. I was a corporate "lifer" and that was fine. I had no reservations about that. I might have even embraced it a little more tightly than some of the people around me because I had felt so cut off from everything during those lonely, depressing years down in Houston.

But the serpent was always there, in the garden, even if I wasn't aware of its presence. Things had been so good for so long that when they began to fall apart, I didn't notice. And, then, I didn't care.

It happened slowly, at first, and then it moved with a kind of terrifying speed. I went from being a little bit too animated and energetic and talkative, to pushy and aggressive and impulsive, to out-of-my-mind manic. Then, psychotic. Then ... suicidal.

It began, I realize now, when I entered into a relationship with a young woman who lived in the house next door to mine. She was in her twenties and a real child of the 60s. I was older. Not that much older but of a different generation. I'd been in the military and that experience soaked deeply into my character. She was a free spirit, to say the least. I was a creature of the corporate culture of the 50s. She was a flower child and into spontaneity. I was a Catholic, though very much lapsed. She had no use for religion. She was put off by the idea of big corporations and wanted me to leave the *Digest*.

But we were having this passionate, emotional affair and I started thinking that this was the big love of my life. And as things got more and more intense between us, I began to lose my grip. She was pressuring me to leave all the things that made up my life—my religion and my career—and become the free spirit that she was and wanted me to be. I wanted to do it and I didn't want to do it. I thought I was in love and that made everything worth it. But I wasn't just crazy about this woman ... I was crazy for real. I was cracking up. I still had my job at the *Digest*.

To anyone who has read the academic, medical studies on bi-polar disease, my behavior was textbook. To those around me, the symptoms were, at first, more irritating than alarming. I started talking a lot and with an excessive amount of confidence that what I was saying was brilliant, insightful, and something that everyone around me needed to hear. There was an aggressive, almost belligerent quality to my monologues and speeches. I was an insufferable know-it-all to everyone but myself. Because ... well, I really was starting to believe that I *did* know it all. I loved listening to myself talk. I was riding a wave of pure self-confidence.

There was a lot of wild energy behind the talking. Behind my every act. I was sleeping very little. Didn't feel I needed to sleep. Waste of time. And, I was drinking a lot but without getting drunk. I felt like I could stay up for hours and hours, knocking back glass after glass of whiskey, at no cost to my brilliance or insight.

And this was merely the early stage of things.

My behavior grew more and more erratic. While I was making good money, I wasn't rich. But I spent like I was. I bought expensive jewelry for the woman I was seeing. Emeralds. Green had a kind of special significance for me that later on became utterly delusional. And, since I was so completely confident about my own brilliance, I decided to become a consultant, while also keeping my full time job at the *Digest*. I opened an office in Chappaqua. And, also, one in Manhattan, of all things. Like I was just going to waltz down and take New York by storm. Like there wasn't anyone there with Steve Millard's kind of talent and insight.

Of course, I didn't have any clients or any leads on finding any. But I had an office in one of the most expensive real-estate markets in the world. I'd go down there, to that office, and if there wasn't anything going on—and there never was—I'd wander around and find a pick-up basketball game on a playground somewhere. Me, a short white guy from he suburbs, playing with these black city kids and mixing it up like I was one of them.

My consulting business did, somehow, generate a single client. One. I don't remember how he found me. What I do remember, to my shame, is that I designed a sales campaign that used some of the most expensive printing products and techniques available back then and that I cost him an arm and a leg and didn't bring him anything like the business it would have taken just to cover the costs of that printing job.

But I didn't care. I thought it was a great campaign. Brilliant. I thought I was a genius and I felt great. When someone would try, gently, to talk me down or get me to "see someone" or suggest that I had a problem, I'd wonder what they could possibly have in mind and I might just tell whoever was trying to help me to go to hell. Because I felt great. I wasn't merely happy. I was way beyond that. I was on a high like I had never experienced before or, mercifully, since. I wanted never to come down. I believed this was my real, true self.

So I was psychotic. Out of control. And, then, I became delusional. I woke up at home one morning after the usual two or three hours of sleep and I began to feel this warm sensation in my lower extremities. Then, it became a wave moving up my legs and then over my entire body. That's when I became aware that I was a modern day Redeemer. I had now swung into a full-blown, delusional psychotic state and had virtually no touch with reality.

Here's how it worked. There was God. And there was the Holy Spirit. And there was … well, *me*. Old Steve Millard, the Redeemer. I had a mission, even though I'm not sure what it was. But I took to writing things down in green ink—mystical stuff that was mostly nonsense—and drawing a symbolic triangle on these pages of notes. The triangle was my symbol for the trinity and I was one of its arms.

I was getting in deep. Very, very deep.

But I did not realize how deep or how dangerous the waters were. It was too exhilarating.

Nobody, of course, could talk to me. Frank tried to get me to "see someone" and I went, once, to visit a psychiatrist in Mt. Kisco. After 15 minutes in his office, I walked out.

But for some reason the people who should have given up on me—who I'd given every reason to just write me off—didn't do it. And I'll never be able to repay that debt.

Frank hung in with me and, like I say, tried to get me to see someone. He also moved me to a job where he thought there would be less pressure and that maybe I'd come around. But I hated the new job and the person I answered to and one day I walked into his office and called him a lot of names and then walked out and slammed the door behind me, feeling like I'd really put him in his place.

Alan Yassky never gave up on me, either, even though one day, when we were fishing the Willowemoc, I told him that I truly believed I would be visited by Abraham Lincoln on his birthday. I'd always been fascinated by Lincoln and had read several of the biographies. It is ironic, I suppose, that the historical figure I found most interesting, even then, was a fellow bi-polar sufferer, a man who never carried a pocket knife because he thought he might use it on himself and who had once taken to his bed for months because of a broken engagement.

Alan treated my announcement like it wasn't anything out of ordinary. "Sure, Steve," he said, "and I'll bet you and Abe will have a lot to talk about." Or something like that. He knew enough not to challenge me in my delusional state. But what I didn't know was that he and his wife, Jean, were terribly concerned and they were talking about how they could rescue me.

Of course, I didn't want to be rescued. I wanted to speak with Abraham Lincoln, redeem the world, be a consultant with an office in Manhattan …

I may have still wanted to marry the young woman but maybe not. We had broken up, at some point, and then I had started having an affair with her widowed mother! So much had piled up so fast. In less than six months, I had gone from being a normal middle-management executive at one of the great American institutions to a delusional, psychotic, and completely out of control basket case.

Things, of course, could not go on at the *Digest* and Frank found a way to ease me out. He persuaded me to resign in a way that insured there would be some severance money and even the possibility that I might return to work some day if I would agree to hospitalization. I think that somehow, even in my grossly delusional state, I realized that this was a good deal for me and that I needed to take it.

Frank and the guys I had worked with so happily for almost five years put on a farewell dinner for me. I'm sure none of them were especially sorry to see me go but I think they all felt badly for me and were baffled about how I'd changed from one of the boys into this madman that none of them knew or recognized. I got very drunk at the going away party and said a lot of stupid things and then I crashed my car into a tree on the way home. The cops came and instead of arresting me, they got me back home.

A few days later, I experienced the inevitable and very real crash when I woke up one morning feeling a sense of depression that had true, physical weight. So much so, that I could not even get out of bed. Could not do anything at all. As high as I had been for the previous five months, I was that low now. My whole world was dull, leaden, and lifeless and gray and I felt all used up. I had entered the textbook next phase of manic-depression.

CHAPTER 12

CHAPTER 12

Depressed.

When I think about it now, the word seems hopelessly inadequate as a description of what I experienced after I'd flamed-out and crashed. We've all been depressed and we think of it as a mood. We're blue because of the breakup of a love affair or the loss of a job. We're grieving over the death of someone we've loved. We're vaguely sad because it is Sunday and raining outside. But this was different. Different not just in its intensity but also different in kind. This was a physical condition. It was a weight. It was oppressive, unending and, I thought, intolerable. And there was no immediate cause that I could identify. My feelings were not moored to any actual symptom; they had a malignant life of their own.

This kind of deep clinical depression bears down on you so remorselessly that it squeezes the normal joys and sensations out of your life and you feel, finally, nothing but its crushing weight. You lose your appetite. You lose your ability to laugh and take pleasure in the company of other people. You lose any interest in sex or work or much of anything. You even lose your ability to appreciate color. You may notice different hues but there is no interest or delight in them. Everything might as well be gray. You feel, at the beginning

81

of a day, that the simple act of getting up and brushing your teeth is just more than you can manage. Taking a shower is beyond question.

These days, most people understand that this kind of depression is a real and dangerous—even deadly—medical condition, even if they haven't experienced it themselves. But back then, many people would write off suffers of depression as people who were simply self-indulgent and weak and conclude that what they needed to do was buck up and pull themselves together.

And to the extent that I was able to reflect on my own condition, instead of merely suffering from it, I shared that feeling and believed that, in some way, I had brought this on myself. That I deserved it and that it might even be a kind of punishment.

People who experience this kind of depression feel "hopeless, helpless, and worthless." And those feelings are self-reinforcing and a tremendous obstacle to overcoming the underlying depression that brings them on.

But it was a while before I learned this terribly important lesson.

For several days, I seldom left my house though there was one time when, in my desperation, I did manage to get away. Not knowing where to turn for help—or even if there was any help anywhere—I called the doctor, Fred Marceau, who had been so kind to me, years before, when I was in Houston. He had given up his general practice and gone back to school for training in psychiatry when he realized how many of his patients' ailments were emotional and not physical.

Dr. Marceau had moved to Monroe, Louisiana, where he was originally from and somehow I found him there. He took my call and listened patiently to what I said. I'm sure he could hear the desperation in my voice.

To my surprise, he invited me down to talk and said I could stay at his house. I responded like a drowning man grabbing for a life preserver and flew down a day or two later.

Dr. Marceau met me at the airport and took me to his home. We spent hours together. He listened while I talked. We even played a round of golf. In the end, there wasn't anything he could tell me that would serve as a magic bullet and make me well. I don't believe he thought there was much hope I could be cured. In his mind, I was a schizophrenic and there was no hope. But he was patient and kind and I took some comfort from that brief visit.

When I returned home, nothing had changed. The depression was still there and it was unrelieved. There were many days, I think, when I hardly did anything at all. I don't remember what I ate and I'm sure I didn't eat much of anything and that whatever it was, it was not healthy. I did drink, though. It was a way of "self-medicating," as we say these days, but it was vastly counter-productive. I didn't really get very drunk and certainly never got happy-drunk. But I suffered terrible hangovers, complete with the shakes and feelings of self-loathing. There were nights when I couldn't sleep and thought alcohol would help. But it just kept me awake or, if I did sleep, it was the agitated kind that leaves you feeling even more tired when you wake up than you were when you went to bed.

So my life consisted of days when I experienced a kind of inertial emptiness and couldn't do anything. And, then, nights when I would try to make myself feel better by drinking. I did not succeed, of course. And I didn't realize that this was, maybe, the worst thing I could do. That it was just getting me in deeper.

And that was, finally, how I came to the point where I wandered out of my house, in the middle of the night, with the Lugar in one hand and a bottle in the other, heading down to the pond where I intended to blow my brains out. This, I thought, would put an end to all this pain ... and that was enough.

But, as I said in the beginning, I didn't pull the trigger. Even so, it was very, very close. For years afterwards, I would take the Lugar out and look at it. I would do this, usually, when I was having a tough spell and needed to remind myself of how much worse it could be.

I made it back up to the house, from the pond, and it wasn't many days later that Alan Yassky and his wife, Jean, came over from Nyack. They came to rescue me; to take me across the river and into their home where they would try to help me get better. If they hadn't come for me … well, I don't know what would have happened. I suspect that I would have been committed to a state hospital somewhere for treatment. Locked up, in other words, until I got better. If I ever did.

So I left Chappaqua and the *Digest* and put myself in the care of my old friends. We'd all gone to the University of Vermont together. Alan and I had been in Air Force ROTC together. He and Jean both remembered the Steve Millard of those days when I was what people called, back then, "the life of the party." That was not the person they came and rescued. About as far from it, in fact, as it is possible to get. Still, they took me in. They had four children and like all young families their hands were full, but they brought me into their home and I ate meals at their dinner table, though I'm sure I was pretty bad company. I didn't have any appetite or much to say. But they put up with me, just the same.

I had a little money, in the form of that severance from the *Digest*. And Alan helped me sell my house so I was able to buy a place of my own, in Nyack. It was a dump. One of those old factory-town places that was run-down and completely without charm. My view was of a fuel-tank farm down on the banks of the Hudson River. But that didn't really make much of an impact on me. I was just going through the motions, putting one foot in front of the other. It was a house and I needed a place to live. I'm sure it was a tremendous relief to Alan when I was able to move out of his house, but he didn't abandon me. Not then and not ever.

Alan had a real estate business and he was doing well enough that he could afford to give me a desk in his office and make me one of his agents. So I had a job and a place to go during the day. But I wasn't in any kind of shape to be out aggressively showing and selling houses. I'm not sure I would have been very good at real estate even if I hadn't been in a period of deep depression. As it was, my record was pretty dismal. I think I sold four houses in each of my two years as a real estate salesman. My commissions were in the $400 to $600 range. Years later, Allen said that he thought I was too honest for the business and that on a couple of occasions, I had been showing clients a place and said to them, "You know, you don't really want this house. It's a dump and way overpriced."

And then, I had taken them around to another place, that was in the same price range and was listed by one of his competitors.

So it was pretty plain that selling real estate was neither going to make me rich nor snap me out of my depression. I was just going through the motions and, sometimes, barely doing that.

My other occupation was as a substitute teacher at Nyack High School. I don't know how I first heard about the opening, only that when I did, I signed up with the condition that I would only substitute for the gym teacher. This turned out to be a good move since the school was full of tough ghetto kids who weren't interested in learning anything and weren't used to paying attention to what teachers said. But they played basketball and respected the authority of someone who wore a whistle around his neck which I did.

So I coached them and they listened to what I had to say because I'd played basketball and knew what I was talking about. I never got close to any of those kids but I remember that even in my own distress, I managed to feel a little sympathy for them. They didn't really have a chance. They weren't learning anything at that school where teachers were afraid of their students and there was no discipline in the classroom. I can remember how, at the end of a long, hot basketball game, the kids who I'd been coaching could not take showers because the locker room had been vandalized. The shower heads had been torn out of the wall and the school had shut off the water.

I made $40 a day as a substitute teacher. Between that and the small commissions from the sales I made for Alan, I grossed $4,000 in 1969 and again in 1970. It had been a long, hard financial fall and in my depression, there were many times when I was sure that I would never get back on my feet.

But I didn't give up. I kept trying to find something that would give me some relief from the dead weight of my depression. I didn't have a doctor who was laying out a regimen for me and outlining the steps in a program of therapy. I was on my own; not really thinking analytically but going by impulse and intuition. But I knew I had to do something; that I had to push back.

So I decided to try wood carving, something I'd first gotten interested in years earlier when a woman I was going out with showed me a small statue that she had carved while she was in art school. The statue intrigued me and the idea of being able to make something like that appealed strongly to me, even though I'd never been particularly good with my hands and didn't have any great artistic leanings.

I'd thought about taking up wood carving earlier, when I was in Pittsburgh, during a period when I was feeling some anxiety. So I made a workbench. I figured I'd need that before I could start doing the actual carvings. I bought some plans along with the materials and the tools I needed and I went to work. It was slow going and I made mistakes and had to do things over but when it was done, I had a very good, redwood workbench where I could do my carving. By that time, though, I was over the spell of anxiety and getting ready to move on to the *Digest's* headquarters and my new job, working for Frank Ronnenberg.

Now, in Nyack, there didn't seem to be any question of my getting better—not any time soon—so I made up my mind to follow through and do some carving. I found a rare wood dealer down in the Bronx and bought a block of black mahogany from him. There was a carving in the shop that I liked and I decided that my first attempt would be patterned after that one. Then I went to a place that sold specialty tools and bought a set of carving tools that would fit in the palm of your hand.

As I said, I'm no artist and I knew I wouldn't be able to visualize the figure I wanted to carve, in three dimensions, while I was working on it. So I bought clay and made a model of what I wanted the final shape to look like. And when I had that, I started chipping away—one small cut at a time—on that block of mahogany. Alan Yassky would come in to his office and see me at my desk, silently working away at that block of wood with a pile of shavings at my feet. He didn't mind that I wasn't out showing houses and probably figured that it was better for his business if I wasn't. It took me a year to finish that first sculpture—a contemporary female nude about twelve inches high that was amateurish at best but that I cherish to this day.

While I was working on that sculpture, I had another idea for a carving project, one that appealed to my love of trout fishing. Using a picture from the cover of an Orvis catalog as a model, I carved wood inlays of trout using no paint, only the natural color of rare woods I'd bought from that dealer—zebra wood, teak, paduk, ebony, and several others.

I mounted the trout inlays on weathered barn board and I thought they were pretty good. Some friends actually "commissioned" me to do inlay carvings that would represent fish they had caught. They'd give me the dimensions of the fish and I'd make the carving and when I was done, there would be some kind of payment. This gave me enough confidence to take a couple of the inlay trout carvings down to the old Abercrombie and Fitch store on Madison Avenue where they agreed to take them on consignment.

This gave my self-esteem a big boost at a time when I dearly needed it and I went further and spent some of the little bit of money I had to take out a full-page ad in *Trout* magazine, offering to carve a replica of a memorable fish for any angler who would send in an order and a check. I wrote the copy and it wasn't bad.

Working from your snapshot, sketch or word description of your trout, I first draw the fish, then cut individual patters from the various woods that best match the colors of your trout. Each piece of wood is then cut, whittled and sanded to fit the inlay. Now your trout seems to come to life, as the entire fish is hand-sanded and shaped, and the eyes and the trout spots are cut and inlaid into the original design. By now there are up to 60 individual pieces of wood in your trout inlay—and there's no doubt at all that this trout is your trout. As a finished touch, the trophy is hand-sanded once again, then hand-rubbed with eight coats of luxurious wax. (There are no stains used on the inlay itself—only the plaque is given a light stain of linseed oil.

I'm sure I thought that description was irresistible and that my prices—$70 to $130 depending on the size of the piece—were fair. But I got no orders from the ad in *Trout* magazine and none of the pieces I'd left with Abercrombie's, on consignment, ever sold.

But in some very, very crucial way, that wasn't important. The carving was a profound success and had accomplished something far greater than a few odd sales and earned for me something much more valuable than a little extra income. I had learned, entirely on my own, that the simple act of concentrating on something other than my depression was not only giving me back my self-confidence but was also diverting me from the pain of that depression. By using my hands and mind to accomplish a fairly simple and repetitive task,

I was fighting back and gaining ground. The ambition and effort that it had taken to go to Manhattan and offer those pieces to Abercrombie's and the work that had gone into writing the promotional copy for *Trout* magazine … all that would have seemed insurmountable to me before I started actually doing the carving.

I gradually understood this and appreciated it. I was learning that if I was going to live with this thing, I was also going to have to fight it. For the rest of my life, my challenge would be to not give in and to find ways to cope with this condition and possibly even prevail over it. I had to find something to do so that one hour of idle gloom didn't follow another and another until an entire day had passed with no reason for me *not* to feel depressed since I had not started anything, finished anything, or accomplished anything. When I had gone through another day when there was every reason to believe I *was* hopeless and helpless.

If, on the other hand, I did my carving, then at the end of the day, I could look at the accumulated shavings and the piece that was taking shape out of what had previously been nothing but a block of wood and I could think, "Well, I got that much done today and that's *something*."

It is hard for me to express, adequately, how proud I was—and am—of what I accomplished with those carvings. Not the pieces, themselves, so much but the fact that I got them done and learned something invaluable along the way. This, at a time, when I was alone with my depression and did not have the help of a physician or the relief of medication. I had only my own will and the payoff that came from the simple activity of carving in wood.

So I say to anyone who is suffering now as I suffered then … you can do it, too. Make yourself do something with your hands; anything that has the slightest appeal to you. Some of that depression will leave you, flowing out through your fingertips, the way it did for me, and you'll like yourself a lot more than you did when you were immobilized by your feelings of worthlessness and helpless and you were not doing anything.

I did my no-talent woodworking from 1969 to 1973, my worst years ever, and it helped save my life. Literally. Those lessons that I learned, from woodworking, on my own would become, for me, something much larger when I was introduced to an entire way of thinking—and acting—to fight this unwanted condition, this intruder in my life.

CHAPTER 13

CHAPTER 13

It was a lonely struggle, fighting this disease—this intruder—on my own. I didn't have a doctor—couldn't afford one—and this was before the development of drug therapies for bipolar patients. And, of course, I didn't even have the correct name for my condition. If I could bring myself to think of it by any name at all, it would be the horrifying word "schizophrenia," which I could not bring myself to say. So for the most part, it was just and endless, lonely struggle with a formless, nameless foe.

There were, as I say, things I learned to do that made me feel better and gave me hope that I might, someday, turn my life around and get back to something approximating what I'd had during those wonderful years at the *Digest* before I descended into madness and, then, this depression that had followed me across the river to Nyack.

I'm proud of what I was able to learn and accomplish on my own and I know that I was able to make myself better. But I doubt that I would have been able to do it all alone or that I would have been able to accomplish what I have since those days of endless struggle and depression if I hadn't heard about a program called *Recovery, Inc.*

I think it may have been my parents who first told me about the existence of this group. We were never close, my parents and I, and during this time the estrangement was accute. But they did worry about me and in a letter, they told me about this self-help group for people with mental and emotional problems and suggested I look into it. I ignored the suggestion. In part, because it came from my parents and in part because when you are in a state of deep, prolonged depression, one of the things that goes away is your initiative. Making that first, exploratory phone call seemed like an impossible mountain to climb.

But one day, in a very low period, I decided to make the first step.

Still, even after I'd learned there was a chapter of this group that met in Nyack, it was another few weeks before I finally went to my first meeting. And I did that reluctantly, at the urging of Alan Yassky who was, in those days, the only person I would listen to. He said, in effect, "Hey, you might as well go and check it out. What have you got to lose?"

What, indeed?

So I went, reluctantly and timidly, to an activity room in the basement of a local church and sat on a metal chair, at the back of the room, and said nothing.

The format of the meeting would have been familiar to anyone in Alcoholics Anonymous and, in fact, Recovery Inc. owed a lot to the successful techniques that had been pioneered by A.A. We had a moderator who stood at the front of the room and read a chapter from a book called Mental Health Through Will-Training. The author of the book was Dr. Abraham Low and he was the founder of Recovery Inc. The book was first published in 1950 and it was hardly a sensational success at the time. Dr. Low's idea went hard against the grain of mainstream psychiatric thinking, back then, which was still in thrall to Freud, Jung, and Adler. Dr. Low believed that the techniques of psychoanalysis were far too expensive and time consuming and that even when they did "work," patients tended to relapse. In his work with his own patients, he was looking for everyday, practical techniques that would help people change and come to terms with the challenges in their lives.

So he worked out a set of techniques and a language to go along with them and this system where patients would meet in a small group and help each other out by discussing the material in his book and then some episodes from their own lives that were similar. One of the fundamentals of Dr. Low's system was that you needed to recognize—to "spot"—those things that would push you into a state of emotional distress. You needed to learn how to spot these "triggers," and when you had done that, you were better able to resist an extreme reaction. You could, in his terminology, avoid a reaction based on "temper." They key was in learning how to think properly about these things.

It all sounds simple—even simplistic—when it is described this way. But sometimes the simplest insights are the most profound and the simplest techniques are the most effective. Dr. Low was looking for results and he worked with patients for many years to develop his techniques. He went with what worked and he was changing lives. Including mine.

It started slowly with me and Recovery Inc. I was embarrassed to be at the meetings. Embarrassed that I needed help so desperately that I was sitting among a bunch of strangers and listening while they opened up the way they did. I didn't want to admit that I belonged in the same room with these people but, of course, I did.

Still, for the first three or four meetings, I did not say anything. I might as well have been invisible. But I did listen and what I heard had an enormous effect on me. It wasn't so much what was said—though most of it was very familiar and very moving—it was that there were other people saying it. People who had the same sort of problems I had. They were suffering in the same way I was and for some of them, it was worse. This led me to the realization that I was not alone and there was something in that feeling. It wasn't comfort, exactly, but there was a kind of relief in knowing that other people were going through what I was going through and, sometimes, worse. Even much worse. Knowing this tends to make you less likely to indulge in self-pity, to ask "why me?" and to admit, instead, that life is full of problems and we all have them and that, in the end, you are responsible for dealing with yours.

Also, being with people who are going through the same ordeal you are enduring tends to make for a bond of sorts. I didn't become friends with the people at those meetings. Not, at least, in the way that I had been friends with people at the *Digest*. But there was this sense of camaraderie and mutual support that was good for my morale. I remember a New York city policeman in our group who was so troubled that his superiors had taken his gun away from him because, I suppose, they were afraid he might turn it on himself.

He was an awfully nice guy. Quiet. Almost shy; even though there was this aura of authority about him, like you would expect from a big-city cop. I remember, clearly, going off somewhere for coffee with him after one of those meetings. I was a long way—emotionally, at least—from those evenings after work just across the river, back when I was working at the *Digest* and headed off to some elegant bar for drinks after work.

Anyway, this cop and I went to a little non-descript diner and while we were drinking our coffee, he asked me in a very quiet, almost conspiratorial way, "Do you mind if I ask you something?"

"No," I said. "Go ahead."

"Well," he said, "do you think I have especially bad body odor?"

He was serious. It was clearly something very important and troubling to him.

"No," I said. Which was true. But it turned out that he had this fear—this delusion, I suppose—that he was especially offensive to people because he gave off this extreme odor. And there was nothing he could do for it. He was trying, through the *Recovery* meetings, but it was hard and he was seriously troubled and I wished I could do something that would genuinely convince him he was okay since my answer clearly didn't satisfy him.

I've wondered, often, whatever happened to him.

There was another member of our group who played first violin in the New York Philharmonic and he was also very troubled. Suffering from depression even more acutely than I was. He came to the meetings and he tried but in the end, he just couldn't find the relief he needed and he threw himself in front of a train. We were a fragile little group and that set us back terribly and, in an odd way, brought us even more closely together.

So I went to these meetings even when I'd rather not have. Alan would call, every week on meeting day, and remind me. And once he'd done that, I had to go. After I started going, I never missed a meeting. I listened and eventually took part I the discussions and I read and re-read Dr. Low's book. Some passages I learned by heart.

- If you can't change a situation, you can change your attitude towards it.
- Comfort is a want, not a need.
- Calm begets calm, temper begets temper.
- Helplessness is not hopelessness.
- Endorse yourself for the effort, not only for the performance.
- Have the courage to make a mistake.
- Feelings are not facts.
- Do the things you fear and hate to do.
- Decide, plan and act.
- Anticipation is often worse than realization.

- Any decision will steady you.
- Don't wait to get well to do things; do things and you will get well.

And my favorites:
- Humor is your best friend, temper is your worst enemy.
- The resoluteness of the muscles will overcome the defeating babble of the brain.

That last one can be shortened into, "Move your muscles." This is what I had already learned, through my woodworking, and in a way, this validated the program to my mind. Since I knew that this part of it worked—I *did* feel better when I had spent several hours carving—I was more inclined to believe the rest of it might work, too. So I embraced Dr. Low's principles.

To this day, when I am in one of my down times, I will return to my dog-eared copy of *Mental Health Through Will Training* and re-read those underlined sentences as a way of reminding myself that I can will myself to be well. I recommend that anyone suffering from bipolar disease—or from unipolar depression—get a copy of this book and do the same. Dr. Low wrote the book more than half a century ago so its language and structure can seem quaint and old-fashioned. But the truths about symptoms and techniques for dealing with them are all there and all as valid today as they were when Dr. Low was writing and as they have been throughout history. Shakespeare understood the same thing Dr. Low was getting at when he put these immortal words in Hamlet's mouth: "… for there is nothing either good or bad, but thinking makes it so."

It is true that Dr. Low is not widely known or read. On the other hand, his ideas have been enormously influential and led to the development of something called "cognitive behavioral therapy," which is now the most widely practiced form of psychotherapy in the world. Cognitive therapy is, essentially, a refinement and advance of many of the methods that Dr. Low pioneered and advocated in the 1930's and 40's.

The best popular and contemporary book on cognitive therapy is *Feeling Good* by Dr. David Burns. It is a wonderful book that has helped millions of people, including me, deal with depression. It is full of insights and techniques that were familiar to me, right away, when I read it the first time. There was even a familiarity to some of the language. When I read, in *Feeling Good*, phrases like "overcoming perfectionism" and "learning to make mistakes," I was transported to that little basement room in Nyack and those *Recovery* meetings.

The lessons I learned there have stayed with me and helped me, time and again.

Many years after I first learned about *Recovery* and embraced its teachings, I found myself alone with Christmas coming and a deep feeling of depression slowly and relentlessly taking me in its grip. I knew that I would be visiting my friends Dave and Polly Henderson whom I had known since we'd been in college together. They are wonderful people and it wouldn't be a stretch to call them my best friends. I spend every Christmas with them since I have no family of my own. They opened their home to me and took me in like I was part of their family. It was always a happy time for me, being with Dave and Polly and their children, and I didn't want to ruin it for them or for me. But going to their home, in a state of deep depression, would have done that.

I didn't know what to do, at first, and I thought about calling and canceling and spending Christmas in my own home, alone with my depression. I was a tempting prospect, as giving in almost always is.

But I knew ... knew from way back when I was in Nyack and from all the times since then when I had followed the rules I'd learned in those *Recovery* sessions; knew what I had to do. I had to fight back. Had to move my muscles and accomplish something.

So I decided to decorate the house and the property. It was something I never did, since I didn't spend Christmas at home. But this year, I had to do it. So I drove into town and bought all the things I needed. I bought lights. Lots and lots of lights. Extension cords. Wreaths. Swags. All manner of decorations. Then I came home and got out the ladder and the tools and went to work. I strung lights all around the roof-line of the house and over the door. I put up wreaths and decorations. For two days, I worked on making the house and property look festive and bright, even though my mood was exactly the opposite of that. But the work took my mind off that and the result of the work gave me that magnificent sense of having accomplished something—even though it was just getting the house decorated for Christmas.

When it came time to leave for Dave and Polly's, I was okay. That may be the best Christmas present I ever gave to anyone. And I gave it to myself.

So I look back on the work of Dr. Low and the things I learned through *Recovery Inc.* (and continue to learn from books like *Feeling Good*) as a great gift in my life. I was my great good fortune to find *Recovery, Inc.* when I did and I remain enormously grateful.

If you are troubled by depression and suffer, as I do, from bipolar disorder, I strongly urge you to investigate the program, to try it out and see if it works for you as it did for me. Buy Dr. Burns book and read it. There has been research that conclusively supports the proposition that simply reading *Feeling Good* can be therapeutic. Dr. Burns calls this "bibliotherapy," and I am a believer because I experienced it a long time ago, when I first came across Dr. Low's book when I was at the bottom, looking up for daylight.

Abraham Low Self-Help Systems

802 N. Dearborn St.

Chicago, Il 60610

866-221-0302

http://www.lowselfhelpsystems.org

CHAPTER 14

CHAPTER 14

I learned a lot while I was living in Nyack. Some of it on my own and some through *Recovery, Inc.* and through reading Dr. Low's book. What I learned on my own was that I could find some relief from my depression by simply *doing* something. By "making the muscles move," as they liked to say in those *Recovery* sessions. My woodworking may not have been profitable but it led me to that insight, which is vital to me to this day. *Don't just stare at the wall and let an entire day get away from you so that you'll feel just that much worse for having wasted it. Do something. Move your muscles.* I learned that on my own and, then, *Recovery* affirmed the lesson.

And there were all those additional lessons I learned in *Recovery*. About "spotting," so that you could see a problem coming and recognize its nature and take the necessary mental steps to deal with it. About "temper,"—or what Dr. Burns calls "anger" in his books—and how destructive it is and how you have to recognize it and confront it. I learned those things from Recovery meetings and from my many readings of Dr. Low's book. Learned the lessons and worked to apply the techniques. And it all helped.

But I was still in a state of depression and there was no getting around that. I still had one more lesson to learn about my disease and it was the most important lesson of all.

That lesson came to me one day, in the most routine, offhand sort of way, in the form of one of those everyday remarks that you don't think anything about. As I said earlier, I had been a passionate fisherman since I was a kid and Alan Yassky and I were angling companions. We had fished together right through the worst of my psychotic breakdown and were actually wading a river together, fishing for trout, when I mentioned that I expected to be visited by Abraham Lincoln on the occasion of his birthday. Alan, who was remarkably patient and kind and stayed with me, just said something like, "Well, that's good Steve. I'm sure the two of you will have a lot to talk about."

Since Alan was both a dear friend and a close angling companion, we had shared a lot of stories about fishing and I had, of course, told him about that memorable boyhood trip I'd taken with my Grandfather back deep into the Adirondacks to a place called Ross Pond.

I was sixteen when it happened but even today, I remember it with almost perfect clarity. The trip was that important in my life.

The trip was my grandfather's idea. He was an unusual man and very important in my life. More important, in fact, than my own father.

My grandfather (on my father's side) was just a boy when his father left the family in the 1880's and went off to join the California gold rush and make his fortune. He was never heard from again. So this left my grandfather to support his mother and sister and to work his way through Harvard. Which he did, graduating Phi Beta Kappa. He went into business and he was a success with a chain of shoe stores, so I suppose that is where my entrepreneurial gene comes from. He had five children and 13 grandchildren and I was one of his favorites. If not *the* favorite. Maybe that was because, like him, I loved fishing.

Because he was financially independent, my grandfather was able to spend his summers in the Adirondacks, fishing for trout, and then to return in the fall to hunt deer and bear. He was a serious, devoted outdoorsman and his equipment was all of the best quality, bought from the old Abercrombie and Fitch store in Manhattan. I still have a lot of that equipment, today.

Sometime in the early 1900s, my grandfather and a guide he knew found a pond about three miles off the nearest road and they liked the look of it. So for several summers, they would carry milk cans full of native brook trout into the pond. Those fish spawned and pretty soon the pond had a thriving population of large trout. My grandfather and his guide had their own personal fishing *Shangri La* which he shared with certain close friends over the years.

So in 1951, my grandfather—who was 83—invited a cousin of mine and me to go on a month-long trip with him and that guide to this pond that I had heard so much about and never seen. I don't think I'd ever looked forward to something so much in my life.

My grandfather and the guide had equipment, supplies, and food for a month for the four of us. The wagon and a horse and the guide were waiting for us where a logging road that hadn't been used for a hundred years cut the main road. We loaded up and we started in. It was an easy walk for me. I was 16 and very active in sports and in good shape. But so was my grandfather who walked the whole way with me.

We put up a camp on some cleared ground at the edge of the pond and it was a magical place that felt more remote than it actually was. The pond was surrounded by big timber that had grown back since the time the woods had been logged. Tall hemlock and spruce, especially. The pond was, indeed, full of large and hungry brook trout, which we caught with abandon. We used the old the old classic fly patterns—Parmachene Bells, Royal Coachmen, Silver Doctors—and we caught so many trout that we quickly learned to put what we didn't want to eat back in the water. My grandfather had a rule—if you caught a fish and kept it, then you had to cook it and eat it. My cousin and I ate a lot of trout until we learned to release the fish that we didn't want to eat. I remember one time when we had filled one of those old metal stringers with fish and I was wondering how we were possibly going to eat them all and when we pulled the stringer out of the water, only the heads of the fish were left. An otter had eaten everything else and I silently thanked the otter for the favor.

When we weren't fishing, we were exploring and learning the things you need to know if you are going to spend time out in the big woods. We learned how to build fires and keep them going; how to use a compass; how to identify birds and plants. We watched my grandfather make blueberry muffins in a reflector oven which he put close to the fire to catch the heat and we also watched him carefully cut the maggots out of a large ham that we'd brought in and that we were still eating and using for cooking grease at the end of the trip. My cousin and I learned to drink coffee and we enjoyed it as long as the sugar held out.

Finally, it all came to an end and we came back out of the woods into civilization but I had the best, most indelible memories of my teenage years. A few weeks later, my grandfather went back there for fall deer hunting. After he came out of the woods, he went to bed and died peacefully in his own home. He was an extraordinary man—a hero to me, both then and now.

Well, I'd told Alan Yassky the story of that trip and it had made an impression on him, probably because I'd described it with such feeling. One day years later, he came into the office where I was sitting at the desk, working away at one of my carvings, still in the grip of my depression. And he said, "You remember telling me about that pond in the Adirondacks where your grandfather took you fishing?"

Yes, I said, of course I remembered. How could I forget?

"Well, I think we ought to go back there and do some fishing. Do you think you could find it again?"

And that was it. After almost two years of the bleakest, most enduring depression I could imagine, I was *instantly* lifted up and back into a state of emotional normalcy. I was *excited*. I hadn't been excited, in the least, by *anything* for so long that I had almost stopped believing I could feel these sensations again. But I did. And they were almost overwhelming.

"Yes," I said. "Yes, of course. I'm sure I could find it." And the prospect alone filled me with a sense of true happiness.

So that is how I learned the final and most important lesson from my time in Nyack:

In time, you will get better.

CHAPTER 15

CHAPTER 15

I worked hard preparing and planning for that trip back to Ross Pond. I made lists and bought the tackle and the food and the other supplies we needed. I did those chores with the kind of enthusiasm I hadn't felt for anything in almost two years. We made the trip and while we didn't stay as long as I had when I went with my Grandfather, all those years earlier—it had been a month, back then, while this time it was just a week—we stayed long enough for me to savor the deep satisfactions and pleasures of fishing and being in the woods with good companions. Things I had begun to fear I might never experience again.

This was not just a brief respite or a lull. I don't know how, exactly, I knew this, but I did. I felt none of the old anxiety. None of the depression that had begun to feel constant. I felt ... well, *normal.*

Nobody knows why—not the doctors and certainly not me—but it seems true that in most cases like mine, the mind heals itself in the same way other parts of the body repair a wound. This is one of the most important lessons I ever learned in my long and continuing struggle with bi-polar disease. And it is a lesson that I often have to force myself to remember. But by forcing myself to remember, I am able to make it through some of the bad times. You can endure pain and suffering if you know that it will eventually end and you will stop hurting, but when you believe that there is no end, then you begin to think of ways to end it yourself. You consider destroying yourself as the only way out. Since experiencing the end of my depression, in Nyack, when Alan suggested making that trip to Ross Pond, I've been able to get through some very low times without ever again considering a pistol as the way to end my pain.

While I was no longer in a state of deep, lingering depression when we came out of the woods and back to the real world of Nyack and the occasional real estate sale or substitute teaching assignment, I was still not as strong as I had been. I felt fragile and tentative and wasn't sure what my next move would be. I had come a long, long way down since my high-flying days at the *Digest*. I wasn't sure, yet, that I was ready to try to re-establish myself in that world or even some pale imitation of it.

Once again, help came my way when I needed it most through the kindness of a friend. In this case, the friend was a man named Ed Mayer who was extremely well-known and respected in the world of direct marketing. Ed was a consultant with an impressive list of clients. I'd gotten to know him when I worked at the *Digest* and because I was on fire for the work, I had asked him a lot of questions and tried to pick his brain and learn as much about the business as I could from him. He liked my enthusiasm, I guess, and took an interest in me.

He didn't drop me after I'd crashed at the *Digest* and I've always been grateful to Ed for that. When I was in Nyack, he would call now and then to see how I was doing. Occasionally in one of those calls he would mention a job opening he'd heard about and ask if I was interested. I'd have to tell him, "No, Ed. I'm not ready yet." And, until that trip back to Ross Pond, I wasn't sure that I ever would be.

Now, when Ed called, it was different. I told him I was better and the first time he mentioned a job possibility, I got very apprehensive and had to tell him, "No. I'm still not ready. But soon."

Ed didn't push it. But he did keep calling and the second or third job that he mentioned was something I thought I could handle. It was with a division of Harcourt, Brace, Jovanovich that specialized in educational material—audio-visual stuff. The office was back across the river, in the neighborhood I had left—in my own mind, at least—in disgrace. I wasn't sure I could handle going back there. But I did it anyway.

I'm surprised, in a way, that I did. For years, I'd lived in fear of exposure; had done everything I could think of to keep what I thought of as a dreadful secret that would ruin me and hold me up to the world's ridicule if it ever got out. I had some kind of mental disease. I believed—and not entirely without reason—that people like me, people with mental diseases, were outcasts. That we were shunned and even despised by normal people. Worse, we were laughed at. Condescended to. Written off as freaks. In a word, we were "stigmatized."

It was worse—much worse—in the past. Today, people are encouraged to talk about their problems with depression instead of hiding them and we see television commercials advertising all the various anti-depression drugs. Celebrities talk frankly about their problems and we have all been taught to understand that these problems do not come from a character defect but are, indeed, medical conditions and should be seen as similar to diabetes and other chronic, treatable diseases.

We know that all this is true and, still, there are people today who become nervous when they learn that someone they know is in treatment for some emotional or mental problem. It is human nature, I suppose, and unavoidable.

It was worse when I first learned that I had this problem. Back then, people did not talk about these things and among some people there was a sense of shame associated with mental problems. My own parents felt this way. So much so, that when I was writing this book and telling my sister about it, she told me that she had never known was bi-polar or had any of these problems. She was younger and we were never close but still … my mother knew and had kept it from my sister for all these years. The only reason could be that she felt a sense of shame. For me or, perhaps, for herself.

At first my own shame was, in a sense, preemptive. I was afraid I would be stigmatized if anyone found out. I had lived in fear that people at the *Digest* would learn that I had this *problem* and that I had been to see that kindly old doctor in Houston to try to deal with it. I don't know what, exactly, I believed would happen if they did find out. Probably that my colleagues would, at the very least, distance themselves from me. And, maybe, that they would actually shun me, the way the lepers were shunned as "unclean" in the bible stories. I'm sure I thought that if my secret were revealed to the world, my prospects for promotion might dry up and I might even get fired.

I realize, now, that these fears of mine were exaggerated. That's not to say that it wouldn't have been uncomfortable for me if the secret of my condition had, somehow, gotten out. It would have been. But the people I worked with were far more enlightened and charitable than I realized. Frank Ronnenberg was understanding and helpful all through my ordeal. Rather than firing me at the first sign of trouble, he did his best to get me some help and find a way that I could stay on at the *Digest*. He went way out on a limb for me and he never stopped being a friend, and he still is to this day. He never treated me—or saw me—as a freak. Neither did most of my colleagues. Most of them were sympathetic and supportive even though, in my psychotic state, I didn't believe I needed the support of anyone.

But that doesn't change the fact that I believed—and believed strongly—that my condition was stigmatizing. Clearly I was exaggerating this in my own mind and maybe I was doing this because I was so afraid of this disease that I didn't understand and couldn't even name. It was, in short, a kind of self-stigmatization and I was projecting onto others my own worst fears and feelings. That's why I protected my secret so fiercely before I had the breakdown and my condition became terribly apparent to everyone around me. After that, the question, obviously, was no longer how to keep the secret.

It was how to face the world.

It wasn't easy, but I went back to work. I took the job with the little division of Harcourt and now and then I would see some of my old friends and associates. Some meetings were awkward and a few were very strained. On one occasion, I was in a store when I saw a couple that I had been friendly with deliberately trying to avoid me when they thought I hadn't noticed. There were a few episodes like this. Not many and none of them dramatic or confrontational. They were painful but what I had been through was worse. Much worse.

The new job wasn't much and I didn't feel like there was any future for me with the company. One of the employees who was with the company when I got there thought she should have gotten my job, so that made things tense and awkward from the start. But it felt good to be working again and I gradually got back into it. Still, I knew that this new situation was just a bridge to whatever came next. I wanted something better but I was feeling more determined than desperate. Maybe that was because after what I'd been through I knew I could stick it out in a bad situation. The Harcourt job was far better than substitute teaching and while there were unpleasant associations and memories around the Pleasantville area, they were not as bad as what I'd left across the river in Nyack. I was ready to move and knew that I need to. But I wanted to be sure I made the right move. I wasn't as young as I used to be and after what I'd been through, I knew there were big risks and dangers out there. I was, if not wiser, then far warier. But I could feel the old urge to work hard and be part of something and enjoy the satisfactions that come with success and money. I'd seen what it was like on the other side of the river and I was determined to leave that behind me forever.

CHAPTER 16

CHAPTER 16

It became more and more obvious that first job after my breakdown was not going to be my last job in life. The work was engaging enough but as I got stronger, the job seemed less and less challenging. I was making decent money—$18 thousand a year—and I had a staff of three people and things went along fairly smoothly, except for the one employee who thought she should have been offered my job and did her best to make my life difficult. But that's the way it is in any office and I wasn't going to let her run me off.

Still, I started thinking about my next move. I wanted a change and I wanted something more and at this point in my life, I had learned that when I was emotionally "normal" and stable, I needed to trust my instincts and, as I said earlier, to be alert for signs. I hadn't recognized any signs—not yet, anyway—but my instincts were telling me that it was time to move on.

My thinking wasn't specific and detailed. There was no step-by-step plan for the future with every base covered, or anything like that. But I had some general ideas. I wanted to stay in marketing. It was what I knew and loved and, frankly, what I was good at. I didn't want to start over in some new field. And, I wanted to get away from Pleasantville and Chappaqua and Nyack and all the unpleasant memories and associations those places still held for me. I wanted to get away but not necessarily to some place I'd never been. Just the opposite, in fact. I was

111

thinking about a place where … well, where I'd been *happy*. New England, in general, and Vermont, specifically. In my mind, those places were associated with the outdoors and fishing, which were things I loved, and then there was the time when I was at the University of Vermont and I'd been very happy there.

So, when I had narrowed down the area, I started my search. And the first job opening I looked into was with the Conservationist magazine, which was published by the state of New York. It was great little magazine and it needed a circulation director. It wasn't Vermont but it was close and any magazine devoted to the outdoors in New York would be covering the Adirondacks, which meant Ross Pond to me and that was one of the places where I had spent some of the very happiest, most memorable, and meaningful moments of my entire life. It was where, in my mind, I had been reborn. So I applied and went up to Albany and interviewed for the job. It was an all-day interview which led me to believe that it was a pretty important job and would, therefore, pay well.

When it was over, they said, "Well, we really want you." And then they told me that the starting salary would be $4 thousand a year.

I said, "What?"

And they said, "Sorry, but that's all we can afford."

I said, "Thanks but that's impossible." And then I decided that maybe I'd better head further north and I wound up in Manchester, Vermont where I applied for a job with the Orvis company and interviewed with the owner, a man named Leigh Perkins who, in one those co-incidences of life, later became one of my best customers and a good friend.

But at that first meeting, I was just another guy who'd come in off the street, looking for a job. I don't remember even having an appointment. But, as it turned out, Leigh had an opening. He was looking for a marketing director. So I had an interview with him and I knew, as we were talking, that things were going well and that I had a good shot at the job. I was excited about that, to put it mildly, since Orvis was all about fly-fishing and especially fly-fishing for trout and in New England. Orvis had been in Manchester since before the Civil War. The company made what were, back then, some of the most desirable bamboo fly rods on the market and I even owned one that I had picked up cheap, second-hand somewhere.

If you were a passionate fly fisherman, like me, then you knew about Orvis. And you probably got the company's catalog, like I did. In fact, I'd copied one of the trout inlays I carved from a picture on the cover of an Orvis catalog.

The catalog was a small thing, back then, probably not more than 32 pages. I had no idea, of course, that one day I would play a part in making that catalog so much bigger and then spinning off several other specialty books as the Orvis mailing list grew from a few thousand people to several million.

I was just looking for a job and thinking that if I landed one with Orvis, that I'd be happy working there. And not just because I would be back in Vermont and involved in the world of fly-fishing, but because I liked Leigh Perkins. He is an extroverted guy, very confident and hearty, who was very damned proud of his company and certain that it was going to go places and do things.

I left that interview feeling confident that I would get the job and sure enough, a couple of days later, I got a letter from Perkins. He said he badly wanted to have me because they needed a marketing director and he offered me the job. Salary: $8,000 a year.

So I'd gone from $4,000 to $8,000 in terms of offers. But the job I was already doing paid me $18,000.

I called Leigh and explained this to him.

"Well, yes," he said. "That's right. But we're offering 'geographic compensation.'"

Which meant ... I got to live in Vermont.

Leigh used that line on everyone and it worked on a lot of people—especially young people who were desperate to get out of the city and get into the "country living" lifestyle. But I'd been through too much, was too experienced and too old to go for it. I turned Leigh down and years later, we had a lot of laughs about that.

So I was still looking for a way out of the Pleasantville, Nyack, Chappaqua triangle. A way, that is, that didn't involve taking a pay cut of more than 50 percent. And that's when I got another sign.

Back when I was getting started with my woodworking, I had bought some tools, of course, and at some point, my name had gotten into someone's system. I was on list of potential customers for specialty hand tools and that list was bought by a company that sold such tools through its catalog. The company was Brookstone.

The company touted itself as specializing in "Hard To Find Tools," and its catalog was small—32 pages, I think, like the Orvis book—and printed in black and white. Certainly not very imposing by today's standards but a real delight back then. And not just for someone like me, who had a real interest in tools and a need for them. Brookstone was the creation of a very wealthy guy named Pete DeBeaumont who was a genius, really. He had a way, in that little catalog, of sucking you in and making you think you needed some nifty little tool that you hadn't known existed to handle a chore you never even thought about.

As an example, he went over to India and bought up whole lots of these long, chrome pincers that were used in hospitals for picking cotton balls out of a bottle full of alcohol. They were quality tools but since they were made in India, Pete was able to buy them for 20 cents, each. Then he put them in the catalog as "The ideal bacon turner," and explained in the copy how you used the tool to reach into a hot skillet and pick up a piece of bacon without getting your hand splattered by popping grease. He charged $2.00, which was a bargain, and sold a ton of them.

Well, of course, I looked at the catalog when it came and I was charmed and intrigued. Especially when I saw the address was somewhere in Peterborough, New Hampshire. I didn't know where, exactly, Peterborough was. But I knew that New Hampshire was right next door to Vermont and that was close enough for me.

So I filed that away, mentally, as something I might want to move on but before I did anything about it, I went to this Friday night beer party at the house of this guy I knew. He was in the same line of work, roughly, and we started talking. I told him that I'd been looking around "up north" and hadn't really found anything.

He said, "Yeah, I've been looking, too." And then he said he'd come across something and, in fact, it was further up north than he wanted to go.

"Some little company called 'Brookstone.'"

So I asked him if he still had the contact information.

"I've still got the letter," he said.

And he showed it to me.

The letter was a month old and it was from Pete DeBeaumont, himself, saying that he was looking for a list manager and asking my friend to come on up for an interview.

"And you're sure you aren't interested in the job?" I said.

"Not at all."

"Well, can I have this letter?"

"Sure. Take it."

The next morning—it was now Saturday—I read the letter over, looking for a phone number. There wasn't one but DeBeaumont had used his home address of in Worthington, Massachusetts, which was one of those towns with a population of about thirty. I found him in information and called the number.

He answered the phone in a very abrupt fashion that I came to know and appreciate.

"Hello."

"Mr. DeBeaumont?"

"Speaking."

I apologized for calling on the weekend and then I got right into it and said, "I have this letter that says you are looking for a list manager."

"I wrote that more than a month ago," he said. "You didn't answer so I assumed you weren't interested."

So I explained that the letter hadn't been sent to me and how I had come to get my hands on it and that I was interested in the job if it was still open. I imagine I said it all very quickly so he wouldn't have a chance to interrupt or hang up.

When I finished talking he said that, yes, the job was still open if I was interested and willing to come up for an interview. And then he said, "Do you have any references?"

Well … I held my breath for a few seconds and then, since there wasn't any way around it, I gave him two names: Frank Ronnenberg and Gordon Grossman, who was then President of the *Digest*. And I gave him their phone numbers so he could call them right away.

I had no idea what Frank and Gordon would say and calling them to ask them to give me a recommendation … well, that was out of the question. They both knew the best and the worst of me. They had seen me when I was at the top of my game and they had seen me when I was flat-out delusional.

I gave DeBeaumont my phone number so he could call me back and I hung up thinking, "Well, it is out of my hands."

And I waited for him to call me back.

I don't remember, all these years later, being especially nervous about the call. I had, by now, become something of a fatalist. And, plainly, something of a gambler. I had a job that was safe even if it wasn't exciting. I didn't need to go off to a new place and start a new job with a very new company that might, or might not, survive. In fact, there was every reason for me *not* to leave my safe job. The memory of my psychotic break and the two-year depression that followed was painfully fresh. I did not, of course, want to go through that again and I was intuitive enough about these things to know that a radical change in my life might well trigger another episode. I had every reason, in short, to be fearful and cautious.

But, then, I had every reason to be the other thing. To be bold and take chances. I was back to "normal," and I wanted what I had always wanted—success and excitement in my work. I wasn't going to get it by playing safe.

I said it earlier and I'll say it again, now. I can't say it enough: If you are like me and have been dealt this bi-polar hand, then you *must* take advantage of the good times, of those periods when you are not in the grip of the disease. Some bi-polar patients spend their lives playing defense and I understand and sympathize. But if, like me, you crave playing offense, then when the signs are right, you go for it.

I had no idea what Frank and Gordon would say to Pete DeBeaumont. What would happen , would happen. I had made my move and taken the initiative and now it was no longer up to me. Nothing to do now but wait for a return call; if, indeed, one came.

And it did. The next morning. Sunday. DeBeaumont said, "I've talked to both of your references and they say you are fully qualified. When can we you get up here for an interview?"

I didn't have the job at Brookstone. Not yet, anyway. But even if I didn't get it, I had gained something very precious from this unorthodox job search.

Earlier in this book, I talked about my struggles with a feeling that I was somehow stigmatized by my condition. I believed that people not only knew about it but had judged me on the basis of it. In their eyes, I was a "mental case" or a "loony" or whatever. And that was that. End of discussion. I was afraid—and sometimes convinced—that people didn't look at me and see Steve Millard, a capable and industrious marketing specialist. They saw a psycho.

But here were two men who I respected professionally and who knew the good and the bad of me and they were willing to endorse me for my abilities. I realized then—as I have realized many times since—that most people are understanding and affirmative and that, often as not, this fear of stigmatization is something you project onto others. That, in fact, you are harder on yourself than most people are. Those references from Frank and Gordon gave me confidence in myself and in the fairness and generosity of others. And those two things, it turned out, were to carry me a long, long way.

It began with a trip up to Peterborough for an interview with Pete DeBeaumont and the Brookstone team. It turned out to be a strange interview. But, then, I had a history of those.

CHAPTER 17

Getting back to my phone conversation with Pete DeBeaumont on that Sunday morning. I was, of course, elated by the endorsements from Frank Ronnenberg and Gordon Grossman, so maybe I was feeling a little full of myself. Because when Pete said that he'd like for me to come up for an interview, I said, "Well, Mr. DeBeaumont, I'd really like to talk with you but I don't want to waste your time or mine. So I might as well tell you, right now, that I'm not interested in merely being a "list manager." If I go to work for you, I want to be responsible for all marketing. I need to be "marketing director."

"I don't know," DeBeaumont said. "Because that's *my* job."

"Well, I don't want to do just list work. I need to have the whole package."

He thought about that for a minute and then he said, "All right. I suppose we can talk about that, too. When can you be up here?"

I thought maybe later that week would be fine. And I said, "Well, when do you need me?"

"How about tomorrow?"

"All right," I said. "I'll take the day off tomorrow."

So that Sunday afternoon, I drove up the Taconic into Vermont and on through the Green Mountains, and it felt like I was leaving a whole chapter of my life behind. Maybe whole volumes. Things were moving fast but I liked that. For a long time now, things had been barely moving at all in my life and I was ready to get back in the action. That evening, I checked into a little motel that overlooked the Vermont, New Hampshire line. I had dinner alone and I had this feeling that, when I crossed the Connecticut River, I might be leaving an awful lot behind. Some of it good. And a lot of it bad.

In the morning, I went on to Peterborough to the address Pete had given me and pulled up in front of a five-story building with a sign on the front that said, "American Guernsey Cattle Association."

I thought I had the wrong address but when I asked this woman coming out of the building, she told me, "Oh, no. You've got the right place. Brookstone is on the 5th floor."

So I climbed the stairs to what was a big open area where all twelve people in the company worked and everything happened. And I mean *everything*. The catalogs got laid out here, the orders got handled, and the packaging got done. It was a very busy place and the only private space was a little glassed-in cubicle, which was the office where my interview would be held. This was a long, long way from the *Digest* where I had consulted with a decorator on what color scheme I preferred for my private office and where I had a view of the ivy covered walls and ate lunch in a dining room where Stouffers did the catering. But I wasn't put off by this. In fact, there was something really appealing about it. This operation was new, young, and lean. Just right for someone, like me, who was starting all over again.

By now, I felt what a gambler on a hot streak must feel. Everything seemed to be falling neatly into place for me. For a believer in signs, this was a bonanza. One sign had followed another. Finding myself on the mailing list for that catalog ... then getting my hands on that letter ... those favorable references from my old bosses at the *Digest*. I kept drawing winning cards and it was a wonderfully giddy feeling after going through all those months and months of nothing but bad hands. I went into that little glassed-in office for my interview cocky and confident and at the same time, feeling like I had absolutely nothing to lose.

I was talking with three people. Pete DeBeaumont who owned the company, Rick Chollet, who was the office manager and actually ran things on a day-to-day basis, and Debeaumont's wife, whose name was Deland. The interview got started in the usual way and everyone was slightly guarded and tense. Pete and Rick asked me a question or two of a kind of general nature and I answered them. We were just going through the ritual, at this point, when Deland who hadn't said anything, spoke up. She was sitting to my side and I had to turn to face her.

"Mr. Millard," she said, "are you married?"

"No ma'am," I said. "I'm not."

"I see," she said. And, then, someone else asked another question about my background or something and the interview went on.

A few minutes later, Deland spoke up again and said, "Mr. Millard, are you engaged?"

"No," I said, turning just slightly in her direction. "I'm not engaged, either."

She nodded and the interview went back to other things. Until a few minutes later when she said, "Well, Mr. Millard, do you plan on getting engaged?"

"No," I said, and I turned myself fully so that I could look her directly in the eye. "Not at the moment. But if you're trying to ask me if I'm queer, I can assure you that I am not."

(These days, the word would be "gay," and she probably wouldn't ask the question. But those were very different times.)

It was an impulsive answer but I was feeling impulsive—and confident. Answering that question that way was eerily reminiscent of the way I had handled that stress test, years before, when I was interviewing for my job with the *Digest*. I was prepared to be respectful but I wasn't going to grovel and I think that impertinent answer to Deland DeBeaumont's question may actually have been the thing that sealed the deal for me in that interview. Pete and Rick both laughed at the answer (Deland and I would laugh about it later, many times) and now that the ice had been broken, we moved on to talk more about the job and about marketing strategies and responsibilities and how the company worked and all the things you would expect. It was good talk and we were plainly on the same wavelength.

Then, it came time to discuss salary and I said, "I need to make eighteen thousand a year. That's what I'm making now and I can't take less."

I could see Rick and Pete kind of recoil when I said this.

"Well, you know," Pete said, "we're a small company and we're just getting started. That seems a little high."

"I understand," I said. "And I'm not trying to be greedy. I don't need to make any more than I'm earning now but I don't really see how I can make a move and take a pay cut."

Pete and Rick both nodded in a non-committal way. As though they understood the logic but weren't sure they could handle the economics. And we left it there.

The interview came to an end and Pete said he would be in touch. Nobody said anything about dinner or a drink, so I went back down the stairs, got in my car, and drove home. It was a three or four hour dive so I had plenty of time to think. I suppose I could have done a mental post-mortem on the interview and tried to figure where I'd given the right answer or the wrong one. Where I had impressed the people I was talking to and where I had blundered. I could have reconsidered my flip answer to Deland DeBeaumont's question.

But I didn't dwell on any of those things. At this time in my life, I was content to take things as they came. I had been taken down and nearly destroyed by something that I had no control over, did not understand, and could not even name. And now, through a series of implausible coincidences I was looking at the possibility of a new start in a new place. But I felt no apprehension. No nerves. Things would work out the way they worked out. Worrying wouldn't change things, one way or the other, and I'd had enough of worrying. I'd know soon enough if there was a new life for me. For now, I drove the winding two lane through the winter mountains and enjoyed the view.

If I had been worried, it would not have been for long. Rick Chollet called the next morning and offered me the job.

"I've never made up my mind this quickly on hiring someone," he said. I found out later that the money had been tough for him since I was being paid only a thousand or so less than he was. But Pete and Deland DeBeaumont were living in Massachusetts and coming up to Peterborough for a day or two a month and they didn't want to do any more than that. With the company growing, it was either give it more of their immediate attention or hire someone to come in and take over some of things that required more and more of Pete's time. That someone, it turned out, was me. And they were in a hurry.

"How soon can you get started?" Rick said.

I had responsibilities at Guidance and told Rick I thought it would take a couple of months to take care of them and make sure that there was someone in my place.

"Can you make it sooner?" Rick said and made it pretty clear that today wouldn't be too soon.

So we compromised on a month, even though he wasn't happy about it. I started getting things cleaned up at work and leaving behind my life in the Nyack,

Pleasantville, Chappaqua area. Things there had been so good and then so bad that living with the memories was a daily burden and one that I was happy to leave behind.

I needed that month but it couldn't pass quickly enough to suit me. And when it had, I loaded the car and drove, again, up the Taconic and through the Green Mountains. I was leaving a lot of baggage behind and that felt good. But there was one thing I knew that I was *not* leaving behind.

And since there was nothing I could do about that, I did not think about it.

CHAPTER 18

CHAPTER 18

When I moved up to Peterborough and took the job with Brookstone, I felt I was truly starting over. If I hadn't exactly been to the top at the *Digest* I had been close enough to the top to look up and *see* it. This was the pinnacle of a world that I found fascinating and seductive and where I had hoped to succeed and spend my entire professional career. Then, with no warning, that dream had vanished as I descended, literally, into madness.

Now, I had come back. Slowly, tentatively, and on my own until I was strong enough to take some risks and get back in the game. But going to Brookstone, after the *Digest*, was like entering an alternate universe. I was going from one of the great, established, prosperous American enterprises to a tiny, obscure, hungry startup. If I had been a big league ballplayer, I would have been a starting pitcher for the Yankees who'd lost his stuff and was moving all the way down to a class D club in Georgia.

Except that I didn't feel that way about it. Not at all.

First, I was grateful for the second chance. We don't all get one of those in this life and even back then, I realized that. My epic fall had taught me humility … among other things.

But I was more than grateful. I was also excited. I may not have been as young as I once was but I still felt the kind of enthusiasm you feel when you are a kid taking a chance and thinking, "What the hell. I'll *make* it work."

After all, what was the worst thing that could happen to me? The company could fail and I'd be out of a job. That didn't seem like such a big deal any longer. I'd just been through a lot worse than that.

And, I think, because that experience was so fresh and so terrible, I was able to keep the risks of going with Brookstone in perspective. And—not to get too complicated about it—this kept me from feeling the old nameless anxieties and dreads that were a part of my condition. A part of this illness I could not name.

I believe if I had been going into another big, established company like the *Digest*, the pressure may have been too much for me. When you are working in a successful, prestigious organization, with capable, confident people all around you, what you feel is a constant fear that you might not measure up. But if you are with an outfit like Brookstone was when I started there—small, lean, and hungry—you feel like you are part of a team and that you are all in this thing together; that you will succeed or fail as one. You tend to lose yourself in the challenges and the work and that, of course, is one definition of happiness. Embracing something larger than yourself.

Which I did, right from the start. I got a small furnished apartment in Peterborough, moved in, and lived there until I found a house to buy. Then I went to work. For the next five years, except for time off for fishing, I worked seven days a week. I hardly thought about anything *except* work. I did enter into a relationship with a woman and it was good for both of us without ever reaching that point of intimacy and commitment where I began to feel the kind of anxiety and loss of control that had been so disastrous for me back when I was at the *Digest*.

I never really wondered, at the time, why I threw myself into the work at Brookstone the way that I did. It just seemed like the thing to do. But now, with time to reflect on it, I think there are a couple of reasons. One of them had to do with the work, itself, and the other had to do with me and what I had learned through experience and through those arduous but priceless *Recovery Inc.* sessions back in Nayack.

Taking that one first: one of the essential lessons that Dr. Low stresses in his book and in the *Recovery* program was summed up in this rule—*Move Your Muscles*. The worst thing you can do when you are in a state of depression is … nothing. The days when you never get out of bed or, if you do, when you never accomplish anything more than staring at the wall or the television … those days compound the problem. They make things worse because the underlying sense you have of yourself when you are in a state of depression is that you are hopeless, worthless, and helpless. Spending the day sitting in a chair and staring at the wall merely confirms this bleak judgment. You are, indeed, helpless, worthless, and hopeless. Hell, you've just *proved* it.

As I wrote earlier, I stumbled onto this insight on my own when I took up wood carving. At the end of the day, I could look at the pile of shavings on the floor and the evolving shape of the project and know that I had done *something* with my time; that the day was not a total loss. This made a difference and kept me from slipping back, further and further, until I was thinking, again, about putting a pistol shot into my skull.

The *Recovery* sessions and Dr. Low's book supplied professional confirmation and made me believe, even more strongly, in the "move your muscles" rule. And, now, many years later, Dr. Burns, who wrote the standard popular text on depression, *Feeling Good*, confirms it yet again. I will have more to say, later, about all this. About how my own experiences have validated the medical, professional insights of these two experts and how they can help other people suffering from bi-polar disease. But for now, leave it that I had been conditioned by my own recent experience to throw myself into the new job at Brookstone.

And the job, as it turned out, was a perfect match for my kind of desire. Which brings me to the second reason I was able to throw myself into my work. That job was, to put it simply, just an awful lot of fun.

There were no bureaucratic barriers to what I could do. I was, nominally, the guy in charge of marketing but the fact was, at Brookstone, everybody did everything. The catalog described itself as the place to go for "Hard To Find Tools." But before we could put them up for sale in the catalog, we had to find them ourselves.

So we all traveled around, going to shows and looking for neat little devices that we thought would work for the catalog. Pete Debeaumont did a lot of this and he was great at it. He just had a kind of a knack. And he had hired an engineer who also went around scouting. But all of us did some buying and I got into it on the fishing and outdoor end of things. It was fun looking around and finding something you were just sure was going to be a big hit with our customers and bringing it back to the office where it would go onto a big table and the five us who made the decision would stand around expressing our opinions on what would, and would not, work.

That's the way it was done. We all found things and we all participated in the decisions about what would—and would not—go into the catalog. When I first got there, Pete Debeaumont was plainly the best at picking winners. But as we grew, he fell back a little and the rest of us got better until we were all 50/50 on winners vs. losers.

Once we had decided that a particular item was going into the catalog, that was just the beginning. Now we had to sell it. This meant taking the right photograph, coming up with the right headline, and writing copy that would convince the person reading the catalog that he just had to have this little gizmo. That his life would be somehow incomplete until he held it in his own two hands … and that at our price it was a great bargain.

Then, once we had decided on the steak, it was time to add some sizzle.

This was my job but, again, because we were a small, intimate outfit, everyone was in on it to one degree or another. We weren't hobbled by the kind of turf wars you see at bigger, more established outfits. We didn't have the time for them.

At first Pete Debeaumont stayed on top of this part of the operation and this was a good thing. He had a feeling for the company and its personality. It was his baby, after all. He would read and edit copy and there was one editorial comment he would use over and over. If you put in some language that was nice and flowery but didn't really mean much of anything or do a very good job of describing the product or telling the reader why he really needed to buy it, Pete would write in the margin of the page, "Cute but meaningless."

You didn't want to see that because … well, he was almost always right.

There were, of course, some items that no amount of skillfully written copy could sell. I still remember this paint sprayer that was a real dog. We spent a lot of time dealing with returns of that turkey because we had made a guarantee to our customers that if they were not satisfied with one of our products "for any reason or no reason"—those were Pete's words—then they could return the product and we would refund their money free of charge. It was a first in the industry and we got a lot of people asking how we could do that. Most other outfits would accept returns of defective products, like that paint sprayer, but they drew the line there. We said that there didn't have to be anything *wrong* with the product; it was good enough for us if you'd just changed your mind about it. Our competitors thought we were going too far, that we'd get ripped off, but it worked and it made for a stronger relationship with our customers and strengthened their loyalty to us.

I can remember only one time when someone tried to take advantage of that guarantee. We carried this little glass-cutter that sold like crazy. It had a plastic handle with a diamond embedded in it and it ran for ten or fifteen bucks. This one guy sent it back and he had obviously dug the diamond out. I called him up and said, "We've never done this before but in your case, that guarantee does not apply. You went after that thing with a hammer."

I was mad … mad as hell. And he knew it, so he didn't give me any argument. And the funny thing was, he could have sent it back in good condition and we'd have sent him his money. Of course, he wouldn't have had the little diamond. But like I say, that's the only time I can remember someone trying to take advantage of us like that.

The guarantee was a first in the industry but probably not the most dramatic one that we came up with. That would have been same-day-shipping. We started that a couple of years after I signed on with Brookstone and it was a big winner. When consumers want something, they want it immediately and that was one of the drawbacks with mail order. You had to wait. But by promising same-day-shipping, we were able to give the customer the sense that things were happening as fast as they possibly could. I remember getting a call from Leon Gorman, the CEO of L.L. Bean about that. He wanted to know how we could possibly make it work. I explained it to him and, like other big names in the business, Bean was soon promising same-day-shipping like we were. Everybody was studying what other people in the industry were doing and then copying those things that worked.

Leon Gorman, by the way, became a good client when I started my own business. And also a good friend. But that's for later.

Now, back to Brookstone and what we were doing to make the business grow. Like I said, we knew what the unsuccessful products—like that paint sprayer—

were and, naturally, they came out of the book. The winners stayed in. This was elementary. We could refine that a little by giving the bigger winners in one edition a little more copy in the next. That meant using slightly less copy for an item that was selling okay but not setting the world on fire. We would resize photographs. Play with type sizes. We did a lot of things with the catalog. Some small and some large, like going to color covers which was a very big deal and increased circulation and sales in a big way.

Our business was growing rapidly and that was exciting and it made all of those things we did with the catalog challenging. You are happy to be growing, of course, but you are never satisfied that you are doing everything you can. But if we had *not* been growing, all those things we were doing and trying would have seemed like desperate moves. There was none of that. We made mistakes but we learned from them and we didn't let them get us down. Success is a wonderful thing, that way, and when you are as successful at what you are doing as we were at Brookstone ... well, it just doesn't seem like work.

It was exciting. Hell, it was *fun*.

That Brookstone was successful was undeniable. But it wasn't just our operation that was growing rapidly. We were part of an industry that was on fire. Direct marketing had come into its own, for several reasons, and it was like an old frontier gold rush where new people were coming in so fast you couldn't keep track of them and while many, if not most, of them were either going broke or just barely getting by, some of them were striking it fabulously rich.

This boom was made possible by widespread use of credit cards and 800-number telephone calling. Catalog shopping had been around for a long time but in the past it had entailed picking out the item you wanted, then sending in your order, along with a paper check, and then waiting for the package to arrive in the mail. All this took time and was not exactly conducive to impulse buying.

But with the credit card and an 800 telephone number, you could browse a catalog and if you saw something you felt like you just had to have, you picked up the phone and gave someone your credit card information and, with same-day-shipping—the thing was on its way before you even had a chance to reconsider. Later, overnight delivery by Fed Ex and, later, its competitors, made it seem like you were getting the product almost immediately.

Now, this was before the advent of the mall, so as more and more people moved out into the suburbs, it became easier to shop by catalog than to get in the car and drive into the city to find a store that had what you wanted. If, for example, you were an angler and lived out in the Connecticut suburbs, you could pick up an Orvis catalog and completely outfit yourself for a fishing trip without ever leaving your house. Finding everything you needed within an hour's drive would have been impossible.

So people in the catalog business who had been small—like Brookstone and Orvis and L.L. Bean and Williams-Sonoma—suddenly had an opportunity to get big. Very big. The tools were there.

But we all had to climb a steep learning curve.

One of the things we all learned was that there was a fast way to growth and that was through what we called "list management." If you are in direct marketing, you are sending out catalogs to a certain number of customers. These people make up what's called your "mailing list," and it is your most precious asset.

Your list is your customer base. To grow, which is the goal of any company, you need to add more names to your list. The slow way to do this is to advertise for new customers, rely on word-of-mouth, or to hope that your catalog falls into the hands of someone who finds it interesting and orders something and, thus, becomes a new name on your list.

When you are growing your list this way, you are essentially doing it one name at a time and, like I say, that is the slow route. The faster way, by far, is to get your hands on a list that belongs to another mail order outfit. Even, perhaps, to a competitor. You match up the names, discard duplicates, send a catalog to everyone else and, when one of those people makes an order, you have a new name for your own list. In the crudest sense, this is "list management." It has been refined and fine tuned until it is a kind of deep art involving computers and statistical analysis and all sorts of specialized techniques. Over the years this has become an industry unto itself and several people have done very well at it. Because I got in early, I was one of those.

But, again, that is getting a little ahead of the story.

For now, it is enough to say that while I was at Brookstone, direct marketing was booming and these new techniques were coming into their own. For my part, I was completely involved and absorbed in the business. It was my entire life and I loved it. I was an important player—the marketing guy—at one of the hottest new companies in the industry so, naturally, other people in the business knew who I was and they would call me—the way Leon Gorman had—to talk shop. Soon, I was being invited to seminars and professional meetings where I would participate in panel discussions about various aspects of the business and where I would talk about some of the things we were doing at Brookstone and explain why they worked ... or didn't.

At first, I thought of these conferences and other meetings as a kind of novelty and didn't take too seriously. They obviously allowed me to extend my contacts and I assumed that would help Brookstone in some small way. The more people I knew, the more insights I could get into techniques and strategies others in the industry were using successfully. So there was, potentially, something in it for us.

What I didn't realize until I had been at it for a while was how much doing these meetings and conferences would do for me. We all know about networking and how important it is in business today. Well, going to these events and appearing on these panels was a terrific networking opportunity. But there was more to it—a lot more—than that.

Going back to my days in college and maybe even before that—to the time when I was delivering papers, picking and selling strawberries, or working as a bartender—I had been good with people. I'd always enjoyed the give and take and I like to think I have a feeling for it. I like a joke and I believe I have a pretty good sense of humor. Many friends have told me so and ... well, who am I to argue.

But that long spell of deep depression had shaken my confidence and I wasn't so sure of myself these days, when I was out in public and on stage. It was one thing, back in the office, with my co-workers. They were people I knew, who I saw every day, and if I bombed with them, no big deal, I'd mount a comeback tomorrow. But going out on stage, in front of a bunch of strangers who were, in some cases, business competitors ... that was different. And I approached it, at first, with considerable apprehension.

Turned out, though, that I was good at it. I don't want to sound immodest or vain—and certainly I've already painted a pretty unflattering picture of myself at the worst point of my life—so I'll have to ask readers to take that assertion on trust. It would be impossible to capture the mood at those conferences all those years ago. Even if I could remember some of the things I said that made people laugh, they wouldn't seem funny without the context. But they were very funny at the time. People laughed and made a point of coming up after a program was done and telling me how much they had enjoyed it. One invitation led to another and I did more and more of this sort of thing.

Like I say, there were good business reasons behind my traveling and speaking so much. You can't stress enough the importance of networking these days. The more people and contacts, the more resources and customers you have. That is almost self-evident. But I had lots of powerful personal reasons, as well, for going on the road and doing the conferences and panels.

It was good, certainly, for the ego and even though I had put some time between me and my breakdown and that dismal stretch in Nyack, I hadn't forgotten it. Everyone likes approval and praise. But I think it might have meant more to me than to the average person. I had, after all, been about as down on myself as you can get. Now, people I didn't know, whose only experience of me was sitting in an audience and listening to me speak on a panel for an hour or so … those people were laughing at my jokes and telling me how much they appreciated the things I'd been saying. One appearance would lead to another invitation, or several invitations, and I began to think of myself as a real player in my industry. And I'm not being vain when I say that … well, I *was* a real player.

It is a good thing to feel important and respected. And it is a hell of a lot better than the opposite. Believe me, I've been there. It's like the old line where someone says, "I've been rich and I've been poor and, trust me, rich is better." And I say this not because I want to blow my own horn—not exclusively, anyway—but because I have sincere hopes that this book will be read by people who are bi-polar and who are going through different variations of what I went through. Who are living in their own personal hell.

What I want to tell them is that—*based on my own experience*—I know that if you'll hang in there and engage your illness and fight back, you can come through the dark, bad times and find sunshine on the other side. And when you do, that's the time to trust your instincts and if you have big dreams or goals, then go for them. Take risks. Embrace them. You don't know what might happen. And the worst thing can't be much worse than what you've already been through.

In my case, one thing had led to another and then another until I found myself with a good job in a hot industry where I was becoming something of a star. If you had told me, back when I was in Nyack, doing substitute teaching and pretending to sell real-estate in a job that was essentially nothing but charity from an old friend ... well, even though it was funny in a dark sort of way, I wouldn't have even smiled because I had almost forgotten how.

But I had hung in and with the help of friends, the guidance supplied by *Recovery* and Dr. Low's teachings, and an exercise of will on my part, I had made it. I had come back into the sunshine and now, after following my instincts, taking some risks, and going all in, I was where I was. Successful and happy. It was wonderful.

So wonderful, in fact, that I decided to give it all up and *really* go for it.

At 40, I quit my job at Brookstone and started my own business.

CHAPTER 19

You don't simply decide, one day, to quit your job and then do it on the very next day. Most people don't, anyway. And, while I may be bi-polar, I am like most people in that respect. My decision to quit Brookstone and go out on my own evolved over time. I'd say that I thought about it seriously—very seriously—for around a year. So while it may have been a risky thing to do, I did not do it impulsively. I think that is an important distinction. Bi-polar people, when they are in a manic phase, act impulsively, often with terrible results. That had happened to me, back when I was at the *Digest*. This was different. My condition was not influencing my decision. I was acting— and thinking—like a normal person. My motivations were those of millions and millions of normal people.

I suppose that one of the strongest motivations behind my decision was one that I share with a lot of people. I'd always worked for somebody else and I'd always wanted to be my own boss. I wasn't unhappy doing what I was doing at Brookstone—like I've said, I loved it—but even though I had considerable authority, I wasn't the one making the final call. Ultimately, I was answering to someone else and sharing in the success—or failure—of whatever the project or the enterprise was. Nothing wrong with that. But there is that final, tantalizing prospect of building something that is *yours* and succeeding on your own. Some people have this in their DNA. Maybe most people do. But a lot of them never quite pull the trigger. They wait, they put it off until the kids are out of college or the mortgage is paid off or the time is exactly right ... or something. And then, one day they realize that the moment has passed and that they will have to be content with running out the string and hoping that the 401K appreciates enough that when retirement comes, they'll have the resources to enjoy it.

For some reason, I understood this in an intuitive way. I knew that if I waited and waited, then I might wait too long. I understood—again, intuitively—that there might not be any such thing as the perfect moment. That I would be lucky if I saw a moment that *might* be right and seized it.

I was in my 5th year at Brookstone and my 40th birthday was coming up. If I waited until after I was 40, I thought, then I would probably just keep on waiting and waiting and the thing would never happen. So I had this very urgent sense of a deadline approaching.

I've discussed earlier how I've come to believe in signs; in how seemingly random events or coincidences can point the way for you and that you should recognize these signs and act on them. I don't mean to sound like some kind of mystic or something. I'm not someone who checks the astrology column in the paper or anything like that. But if your antennae are sensitive and you are faced with a critical, fork-in-the-road decision, then you will often get some form of guidance from what I think of as "signs." I know that it has happened to me, many times, going back at least as far as the call from my old roommate in Washington telling me that the *Readers Digest* was interviewing.

So, while I was trying to make what might have been the most important single career decision of my life—whether it was time, indeed, to strike out on my own—a couple of things happened that I considered signs and that moved me very strongly toward the decision I finally made.

First, I got a call from a guy down in Texas who was a "list broker." That is, he helped people in the direct marketing business rent the mailing lists of other companies and he got a commission when he made a deal. The commission was based on the number of names a company paid to rent. This was a new, niche business in an exploding industry. I knew the guy by name and I had talked with him on the phone a couple of times but I'd never met him. He knew me by reputation. Like I've said, I was getting to be pretty well known in the industry and I had a reputation as a guy who understood direct marketing and had a flair for it.

Well, I had business reasons for being in that part of the country, so I made arrangements to meet with him. We got together and it turned out he was looking for a partner and he made me an offer. But first, as a way of tempting me, he let me look at his books and I was impressed. He was doing well. *Very* well. Far better than I would have guessed.

So we talked and I asked him about his background. He told me that before he started doing the list brokering, he'd been a computer salesman. He had no experience at all in marketing. That's why he wanted me.

Like I say, I was tempted. But it also occurred to me, without too much reflection, that if a guy who had no marketing background and no experience actually working in mail order could do as well as he was doing … well, maybe there was some opportunity here. I knew I didn't want to be this guy's partner—for one thing, I wasn't interested in moving back to Texas, a place that was filled with unhappy memories—but I thought I might just do okay as his competitor.

So that was one sign and it got me thinking real hard and actually sitting down and doing a business plan and running the numbers, trying to figure out just exactly how much I would need to have in the bank to do what I wanted to do for one year. I figured that would be enough time to know if this thing was going to work or if I'd have to find another job working for someone else.

I was doing this research at night, after work, and spending a lot of time on it. I was serious now and I wanted to be certain of the numbers. I tried very hard to think of everything and to honestly calculate every expense. I calculated how much I would need to spend for the phone and for travel. For rent and insurance. For office supplies … right down to the last sheet of paper. When I was done, the total I came up with was $50,000 and I'll say right now, for anyone who is looking to me for advice on starting a business, that when you've done your plan for your first year, look at the number you've come up with for how much you'll need … and then double it. I've heard that advice, here and there, on starting your own business and my own experience confirms it. Whatever you think you'll need, it will turn out that you'll actually need twice that much.

Anyway, the figure I came up with was fifty thousand. I thought it was a solid, realistic number. Now, all I had to do was come up with the cash.

Well, as I've said, I'm a collector. It is a hobby and maybe a little bit more than that. Just say I'm serious about it. For this reason, I had some things of value that I could sell and I raised about $25,000 that way.

That was the easy part.

Now, as long as I had been working for Brookstone, I had been looking for ways to leverage whatever money I could save. This was in the late 70's and inflation was on a tear and just putting money in the bank was a way to come out with less—in actual value—than you started with. So what I settled on was … land. I would buy up little parcels of land around Peterborough. Not many. Just three or four and they were not anything grand because I wasn't working with a big pot of money and I was actually just paying 10 percent down and financing the rest.

I'd bought one of these properties from a wealthy widow and paid $20,000—$2,000 of it down and the rest financed, structured it around one payment a year at five percent or so. In those days, it was a very good deal. Well, a couple of years later, just about the time I was trying to figure out how to come up with another $25,000 to start my own business, I got a call about this property. The call was from young couple in town—I knew them—and they wanted to build a house. They thought the property was right for their needs and could we talk?

I said sure. But I didn't know what the property was worth or what to ask for. Like I say, I'd bought it for $20,000 a couple of years earlier. Say it had appreciated, oh, 10 percent. Twenty-two thousand. And I still owed not quite $18,000. Four thousand profit for me but that wasn't going to get me there.

I called Alan Yassky and asked him for advice.

"What's a fair price?" I said.

"Not the right question," he said.

"Okay. What *is* the right question?"

"The right question," Alan said, "is, 'How much do you need?'"

"Well, I'd like, say, thirty-thousand." That number just popped into my head for some reason.

"Then tell them you'll take thirty-thousand and not a penny less."

"I can't do that," I said. "It's not worth that much."

"Yes, you can. And if they are willing to pay it, then that is what it is worth."

"I don't know …"

"Look," Alan said, "I want you to stand in front of a mirror and say, 'I'll take thirty thousand. Nothing less.' Do it until you feel comfortable doing it.'"

During the bad times back in Nayeck, I'd gotten used to doing whatever Alan told me to do, so I practiced in front of a mirror. But I never really felt comfortable saying the words, 'Thirty-thousand. Nothing less.'"

But the next day, when I met with the people who were interested in buying, I said the words and to my great surprise, they agreed to the price. But they weren't interested in financing the deal. The woman had a rich father and he told her not to take out a mortgage, he'd give her the cash. So I had $30,000 in hand.

I went to the woman who I had bought the property from and who was financing me and said I wanted to pay off the loan. She said, "You didn't read the fine print."

I said, "What fine print."

Well, it turned out, she didn't want a lump sum payout and had written it into the contract that I would pay off the loan over some period of time. I think it was 15 years. And that was that. She wanted the predictable income.

Now I was able to restructure everything so I had the cash from the couple who had bought the land from me but only had to keep paying off my loan a little installment at a time.

I had the cash I needed. A little more, actually, than the $50,000 figure in my business plan.

If that isn't a sign, then I don't know what is. It surely went a long way toward making up my mind for me. I settled on a date when I would formally give notice but before that date came, my boss came into my office to talk about something one day and I just couldn't help myself. I was too keyed up to hold it in any longer.

"Rick," I said, "I need to tell you something. I'm leaving."

"Leaving?" he said.

"Yes. I'm going out on my own."

I forget exactly what he said but the meaning was plain enough. He didn't think I would make it on my own. And, to tell the truth, I wasn't sure myself. But I was in, now, up to my neck.

I was, understandably, both excited and apprehensive. Like anyone would be. But bi-polar disease is not something that just "anyone" has to deal with. And this is something I've thought about and that is probably worth sharing. Bi-polar people experience all the same challenges and setbacks that normal people do. The difference is … we have this additional challenge. It is something that is always there and there are people who give in to the fear of it and just give up. They let their bi-polar condition keep them from doing what they could be doing. It isn't the disease that is keeping them back but their *fear* of the disease.

I've tried never to let this happen and I think I've succeeded. Part of the reason for this is that over the years, I found that I could fight back. I learned, for example, to do things to keep from experiencing that awful sensation that David Burns calls "do-nothingness." Then, there were the lessons that I learned with the help of *Recovery Inc.* and Dr. Low's book. How to identify my "triggers" and "spot" them. How to control "temper." How to "endorse" myself.

I learned that things could be "distressing but not dangerous." I learned that boring is okay and that it is all right to be average. Learning all these things allowed me to live a life and to succeed. I still had to tough it out, from time to time, if I wanted to get through periods of anxiety or depression. I'd had to bluff my way through some situations so that I wouldn't be tagged as someone with "a problem" of the kind that people were afraid to call by its name.

And through all this, I have to say, I remained essentially … an optimist. While I don't know what came first—the optimism or the things I learned about myself and my condition—I am certain that an optimistic, hopeful outlook made it possible for me to quit my job and start my own business. With one client, one employee, and $50,000 on hand to make it through the first year.

Being bi-polar is not something I would wish on anyone and it is certainly not something I chose for myself. But it is something I've had to learn to live with.

And learning to live with this condition has, I think, made me into a tougher, more optimistic person than I might otherwise have been. It certainly made me more willing to take risks.

In a way that is almost too ironic, my bi-polar condition actually worked to my advantage for once in my life when I launched my business. No doubt the emotional stress and stimulation of the experience provoked what was a mild, but definite hypo-manic condition in me during these months. It wasn't the kind of extreme emotional state that I been through back at the *Digest*. I couldn't have survived that. Certainly not when it reached the psychotic stage.

No, this was much less violent and dramatic but it was, nonetheless, a definite emotional swing to the upside. I had more energy and needed less sleep than usual. I could work long hours and when I talked with someone, I was animated and persuasive. I could make people believe what I was saying because I believed it so intensely myself. I was a dynamo, full of self-confidence and enthusiasm. This condition came over me right when I needed it most. Because those first months were challenging and sometimes frightening, they would have been emotionally exhausting if I hadn't been in a state of mild euphoria brought on by this condition that I still couldn't name but was, for once in my life, working for me.

CHAPTER 20

CHAPTER 20

The good part of starting your own business is that you are on your own. You answer only to yourself. The bad part of starting your own business is … you are on your own and you answer only to yourself. Or maybe I should say the "hard part." Now, when there is a problem, or a decision to be made, you can't pass it up the line. It stops with you. These days, we all know about stress. We talk about it and we understand that it is a powerful—even dangerous—thing in our lives. We may not have used the world so much, back when I started the Millard Group, but that didn't mean that stress didn't exist and that people didn't experience it. I know that I did.

I started lean. It was just me and a woman named Diane Greely. And without her … well, my story would be entirely different. I can't say enough about Diane and perhaps the best I can do is to simply reprint what I recently put in a letter to her:

Dear Diane,

Over the past 30 years, I've had numerous people ask me about starting my own business. I always tell them about Diane Creely (Blauchette, at the time) who arrived at my door just after the word had gotten out that I'd decided to go off on my own.

You told me that you had been making $13,000 a year in your last job but that since I was just starting out, you would accept $10,000.

Then, you added, "And I'm worth every penny."

It was a brief meeting and I told you I would think about it and get back to you.

Well, I did think about it and I realized that I knew absolutely nothing about office procedures, billing, collecting and all the rest. When it came to the actual day-to-day running of a business, I was a babe in the woods.

In fact, I didn't even know if I could do my own job—bringing in clients.

The numbers, of course, didn't work. I had one client. And he'd said he'd pay me a retainer of $1,000 a month. So I'd be handing most of that right over to you.

But I knew I needed someone who was capable and confident. I thought, "Anyone who can look me in the eye and say with such genuine conviction that they are worth every penny of $10,000 a year must really mean it."

So I called you back that same evening and said, "Let's do it."

I clearly remember a long pause on your end. Then you said, "Don't you want to negotiate?"

And so began a wonderful relationship.

You insisted, right away, on a $500 IBM Selectric and I gave in, even though it was more than I had paid first car. And you were magnificent and

I wasn't entirely aware of it at the time, mostly because you rarely told me about all the things you had done.

The fact is, we both did a great job. My gift of gab brought in the clients (that's all I was capable of!) and you took care of them, me, and all the others that followed. Without your organizational skills, it most certainly would have been total mayhem.

I've told all that have asked about Steve Millard, Inc. what a great team we were. We did things right, Diane, mostly because we were both ignorant of the list business and, consequently, never developed any of the bad habits of the other brokers.

The early years were, without a doubt, the most fun for both of us. You had your radio, your beer for lunch, that luxury IBM Selectric, and you were making more money than your boss. So, can I assume you were having as much fun as I was.

When I think about the company, those are the times I concentrate on. The later years were confusing, demanding, and necessary. But those early years were sheer joy for me.

A few days later, Diane answered my letter,

Dear Stephen,

Thanks for your letter last week. It brought a smile to my face and flooded me with memories, too. I still believe to this day that it was meant to be ... though I was unsure and scared to death at the time. I was young, with no responsibilities, so I guess I figured I had nothing to lose … going to work for this stranger I'd met only once, in a brand new company, and in a field I knew absolutely nothing about!!! I still remember standing in my dining room at home talking to you on the phone about the job offer and being incredulous that you wanted to hire me so quickly! My parents thought I was crazy to be driving all the way from Lawrence, Massachusetts (I was living at home when I first started) to Peterborough, New Hampshire each day. None of us even knew where Peterborough was before that time. I loved it right from the get go … and certainly, I loved you from the get go, too. You made it fun and interesting and challenging. You worked hard and motivated me to do the same. And I couldn't get over how you trusted me so completely right off. You were always so supportive and backed me up 100% when I made any mistakes and you were never hesitant to share your good fortune with me or credit me for any good work I'd done. I always have and will continue to be grateful for all the opportunities you provided me … I had a lot on my plate back then (still do) but knowing you were in my corner made it easier.

Love,

Diane

So we had something that I think everyone needs in a small, start-up business … we had a great sense of teamwork, even though it was a very small team working on a very tight budget. For an office, we found space over the local unemployment office which we used to laugh about in a mordant sort of way. "If this thing doesn't work out," Diane and I would say to each other, "we won't have far to travel. We can just walk downstairs and get in line."

I imagine that most startups are like we were—full of confidence in ourselves and, at the same time, scared to death that the marketplace wouldn't agree with that estimate. We got a pretty good wakeup call every time we went by that unemployment office. I suppose it might have inspired us both to work just a little harder.

But, then, as I said at the end of the last chapter, I may not have needed much of an incentive since I was riding the euphoria of a mild hypo-manic state. My unwanted partner in life—for which I still did not have a name—was, for once, working for me instead of holding me back or threatening to destroy me.

So I was coming in early, staying late, and working weekends. My emotional tachometer was redlined and that helped me over my doubts and fears and the normal fatigue and frustrations that I'm sure must make things very difficult for anyone trying to get a new business up and running.

That emotional boost was unbidden. Just serendipity. I certainly couldn't take any credit for it. But there were some things we had going for us that I could take credit for and I'm not going to put on the mask of modesty and say we succeeded entirely by luck. In fact, I'll come right out and say that, yes, luck had something to do with it. But we had a lot more than luck going for us. We had, of course, our own commitment and desire to succeed going for us. And, then, without realizing it, I had been preparing for this moment for two or three years now. Maybe longer. Perhaps even all my adult life and part of my childhood. Those days of selling strawberries when I went around to clients on my bike. The long trips down hot, empty Texas highways on my way to visit another supermarket where I would try to sell the manager on a magazine rack and, if I succeeded, then install it, myself, with my hog ringer. Those brainstorming sessions at the *Digest* during the good times. I had learned the marketing trade from all those experiences. It wasn't formal, classroom training which is to say … it was better than that.

And, then there were the years at Brookstone. I had come in when the company was doing $200,00 a year and five years later, when I left, it was at $25 million and still growing. We had expanded so far and so fast that we outgrew our facilities and had to build something much bigger. I was asked to make some projections on how much we would grow during a certain time frame. The size of the facility we would be putting up would be based on these projections of mine. So I came up with some numbers—not something I'm especially good at—and we bought land, hired architects, and signed construction contracts to build a new facility. Based on my numbers.

One day, my boss at Brookstone said, "You want to go take a look at the new building?"

I'd been too busy to pay attention to what was going on out at the site. I just knew that the new facility was under construction.

"Sure," I said, and we drove out together. When we got to the site and I looked at the building, which covered an acre of ground, I said to myself, "You'd better start looking for another job."

The thing was huge and I couldn't imagine that we could ever use all that space. I just knew that, somehow, I had screwed up the numbers. And maybe I had. Because, in a few months, we were breaking ground for another building of the same size.

So I'd learned that success is possible. No, I'd learned that *enormous* success is possible. And that it can come out of small beginnings. I believe this is an essential component of the entrepreneurial spirit. You don't imagine yourself just doing well and growing by small, steady increments. That may happen but it isn't what motivates you. What you dream of is splendid, spectacular success. You see your business growing so rapidly that you'll have a hard time just managing the growth. You wouldn't endure all the hard work and uncertainty otherwise.

And, then, finally there was the most concrete preparation I'd done. All that networking. All those speeches I'd given. Appearing on all those panels. Making all of those visits to talk with our competitors. These things had given me a name and, I have to admit, a certain stature in our industry. I wasn't some nobody who'd hung out a shingle then sat back and waited for the world to beat a path to his door. People knew who I was and they believed I was good.

And who was I to dispute them?

Kidding aside, I had built a reputation and a web of relationships and when I went out on my own, that began to pay off almost immediately. People would call and say, "Listen, I hear you've gone out on your own. Are you taking new clients? Could you come by and talk to us."

I never said "no" to anyone and I made only one cold call. That was to Williams-Sonoma. And I got the account.

So as daunting as the future had sometimes seemed, I began to get a feeling, very early, that this thing was going to work out. And my confidence began to show and take on a kind of life of its own, separate from the mild euphoria brought on by my hypo-mania.

That realization struck me most forcefully, I think, when I came back from a trip to California where I had taken some prospective clients out to dinner and run up a bill of fifteen hundred dollars. A lot for those days. But I wasn't worried. I was doing it because I knew I was going to land those clients and I wanted them to believe they were signing on with a successful outfit. This wasn't the hypo-mania talking.

This was business.

Well, when I got back to New Hampshire, I found Diane at her desk, crying. The American Express bill had come in and she was convinced that I was spending recklessly and we were going to run out of money.

"Diane," I told her, "don't worry. We can pay it. Everything is fine. We're going to make it."

And I was right. We did make it. We did better, in fact, than I had ever dreamed … even when I was dreaming big.

CHAPTER 21

CHAPTER 21

Earlier I mentioned the old line about how "It is better to be lucky than good." And I suppose it's true as far as it goes. But what's also true is that it is even better to be both lucky *and* good. Especially if you want to succeed as an entrepreneur. There are so many things that can go wrong. So many ways to fail. I read somewhere that only one out of every ten startup businesses succeeds and even then, "success" is not much more than bare survival. Very, very few entrepreneurial visions work out and achieve the kind of prosperity that inspires people to put so much of themselves and their resources into them. There is a lot more heartbreak than glory in this world and this is especially true among startup businesses.

I've already said I was good. And that I don't mean to come off as vain or immodest when I say that. But for anyone reading this book for lessons in entrepreneurship, here is one that is critical: You *must* believe in yourself. If *you* don't, then nobody else will.

I had thought long and hard about the risks involved in going out on my own, with a very close financial margin of error. And I had taken pretty careful inventory of my own strengths and weaknesses. I knew I had skills. I had proved that in my performance at Brookstone and even earlier, before the bad times at the *Digest*. I had worked hard and learned as much as I could along the way and I had met and gotten to know a lot of the right people by going out to the conferences and appearing on panels and doing all the networking that I have previously described. While doing these things, I got the kind of feedback that assured me I was up to the challenge. That I was, in short, good at what I did.

But what about "lucky?"

Well, on the one hand, there are probably some people who, on reading my story, would consider me very *un*lucky. You would have a hard time, after all, convincing anyone that being blindsided by an unnamed affliction that took you to the brink of suicide qualified you as being "lucky." I could probably get a sympathetic hearing from a lot of people if I wanted to argue that I'd been exceedingly *unlucky* and that life had dealt me a rotten hand.

But I honestly didn't feel that way, back then, when I was starting my business and I *certainly* don't feel that way now. To the contrary. I believe I have been very lucky in life. I got some great breaks—landing the job with the *Digest*, for instance—and, even better, I found myself associated with some very good, very smart, and very generous people. And that made all the difference.

For much of my life, I've had to deal —on my own —with being bi-polar. For more than 30 years, I was alone and, more or less, flying by the seat of my pants. I had to learn different techniques and strategies for coping and even surviving. But I wasn't alone in the larger sense. Frank Ronnenberg, for instance, did all he could for me at the *Digest* and gave me a strong recommendation when I was trying to land the job at Brookstone and get away from the unpleasant memories and associations that came with living in Pleasantville and Chappaqua. Alan Yassky took me in and gave me a job when I was lower than I thought it was possible to go. Ed Mayer, the guru of the direct marketing industry, stayed with me and encouraged me during those same bad times. And there were many, many other people who were friends—personal, professional and, quite often, both—who helped me and whose kindnesses I can never repay.

So I had been very, very lucky in my friendships. Lucky beyond what I could have hoped for.

And this continued to be true when I left Brookstone and went out on my own. I was very lucky with my clients, especially my very first one.

My business relationship—and eventual friendship—with Robbie Shipp started the way so many things in this life do. By accident.

While I was still at Brookstone, I had been asked to speak to a group of people who did business-to-business mail order. It was a professional organization and while what they were doing wasn't exactly something I was expert about—Brookstone was business-to-consumer mail order—there were plenty of similarities and common concerns. So when I was asked to give a talk at one of the group's meetings, I accepted the invitation. I figured I certainly knew enough to give a talk and, evidently, it was a pretty good one. As a result of the talk, I was asked to join the group. Then, a couple of years later, I was elected President of the group. I'd like to think it was on account of my good looks.

Well, anyway, I went to the group's various functions including a meeting out in Palm Springs. There was a breakfast buffet one morning and I got in line and when I came to a hot plate that was full of what looked to me like tacos, I helped myself. Then I started looking around for some chili sauce to put on my tacos and that got a big laugh from the other people at the meeting.

Seems I had helped myself to blintzes, not tacos. The group had a large Jewish membership and I got to play the dumb Goyem. None of that kept me from making a lot of friends in the group and, who knows, maybe it helped. What I do know is that I found myself having breakfast and talking with a very smart and pleasant young man who told me that his name was Robbie Shipp and that his father had recently died and left him a business that sold photo albums for business use. It was a good business, he said, and he was making money. But he thought there might be a lot more money to be made in the consumer field. He wanted to pick my brain and we had some friendly conversations that led, very quickly, to our becoming real friends.

Well, we were having one of those conversations and Robbie said, "You know, it doesn't seem right that you should be giving away all this expert advice for nothing. You should be getting paid."

Well, I just nodded when he said that. But the truth is … this came during the time when I was trying to decide whether or not to leave Brookstone and go out on my own. So, obviously, I'd been thinking the same thing he had. I felt like I had the kind of expertise in direct marketing, the kind of feel for the business, that people in the industry would pay to be able to share. But I wasn't quite there yet.

"Have you ever thought about going out on your own?" Robbie said.

I gave him a non-committal answer.

"Because if you ever do, I'll be your first client."

That conversation went a long way toward tipping the scales. Robbie's confidence did a lot to enhance mine. If he was so sure I could do it, then why shouldn't I be just as confident? And, then, there was this: if I did decide to go out on my own, I could be sure I would have at least *one* client.

And that's how it worked. Robbie hired me as a consultant at $1,000 a month and I agreed to fly out to Los Angeles, once a month, to meet with him. Both those arrangements were good for me. I needed money to pay Diane's salary and to cover the rent and to have some cash flow backing up that $50,000 I was counting on to get me through the first year. And making a west coast trip once a month got me to a part of the country where I could meet with other possible clients. It was on one of those trips that I took potential clients to that expensive Chinese restaurant and ran up the $1,500 bill that had reduced Diane to tears.

That dinner, as I explained to Diane, paid for itself many times over. And the relationship with Robbie Shipp brought enormous returns, professional and personal. It made me a lot of money and guided me along a path in my new business that turned out to be exactly the right way to go. And, best of all, it resulted in a wonderful, life-long friendship.

Not a bad outcome to the simple question, "Have you ever considered going out on your own?"

Since Robbie had hired me to be a consultant, it was up to me to come up with ideas that would help him expand the business and make more money. That's what consultants are supposed to do. It's why people pay them. That's the theory, anyway.

Well, one of my first ideas for Robbie struck pay dirt and we still laugh about it. He was selling photo albums to businesses and they came bound in this ugly, industrial-looking plastic stuff. He wanted to sell the same albums to consumers and it seemed like a decent idea to me. But I was troubled by those covers and I remembered how, back at the *Digest*, when we sold books by mail order, we would offer them bound in either the conventional way—heavy cardboard, I guess—or, as a "special offer," you could have your book in what we called "a handsome, leather-like binding." And, of course, we would charge a little more for that. Not a lot more. But certainly a lot more than the cost of that "leather-like" binding.

Well, I'd been impressed back then by the number of people who chose to pay extra for the fancier binding. I don't remember the exact numbers but it was significant and, certainly, more than I would have guessed. By a wide margin.

That stayed with me. It was a lesson in packaging and consumer behavior that I never forgot.

So I suggested to Robbie that he offer the consumer the option of buying an album with a "handsome, leather-like binding." He could charge much more than he did for the album with the conventional binding and it wouldn't cost very much at all.

He was skeptical. First, because he didn't think the customers would pay. He was still thinking like his business customers, for whom everything was a bottom-line decision. If you're buying albums for your business, you don't care what the cover is made of, as long as it holds together, and you aren't likely to pay extra just for make something that looks a little more handsome in the bookshelf.

Consumers, as I explained to Robbie, are different. They often like to show off what they have bought and will pay a little extra to do it. Otherwise, how do you explain designer labels? People who spent extra for the "leather-like" covers on the *Digest* books did it because they wanted to impress people who came into the house and saw the books in the bookshelves. It's human nature. A simple thing. But you can overlook the simple things.

Robbie eventually came around to my way of thinking and agreed to offer the albums with the fancier cover. But he balked at my suggestions about pricing. First, he didn't believe that people would be willing to pay the difference in price I was talking about. Then, he thought the markup I was talking about was just too much. I've forgotten the exact numbers but let's just say that it cost two dollars more to produce albums with "leather-like" bindings. I wanted to add five dollars to the price. My theory was that you had to charge that much to make people believe they really were getting something special.

Robbie thought that was just too much. That it was unfair to the consumer. So he wound up charging, say, three dollars more for the albums with the fancier bindings.

Whatever the price he settled on, it was immediately apparent that I was right about customers being willing to pay more. He sold a ton of those albums with the "leather-like" covers. And, eventually, he came around to my way of thinking about the "right" price and began marking the albums up they way I'd suggested.

That worked, too.

It was simple stuff. Obvious to me, because of my background and experience. But to Robbie, these were very profitable suggestions. They made him a lot of money. Far more than necessary to justify what he was paying me as a consultant. Robbie was happy and it was, as they say, the beginning of a beautiful friendship that endures to this day. Robbie built the business and was enormously successful before he sold out and took a big profit. I continued as a consultant but where I really made my money, with him and with other clients, was in doing list management. That's how I built my business from a two-person operation in a space over the unemployment office, to an operation that employed more than 200 people and billed more than $60 million a year when I sold it.

There were two immediate results that followed on my early success with Robbie. He talked me up to other people in mail-order and that, along with the reputation I already had, led to people in the business referring to me—the way they previously had to Ed Mayer—as "the guru of catalog marketing."

So I started getting calls. A lot of calls. And I followed up on every single one of them and started signing up more clients. This, of course, increased our billings and our cash flow until, one day, Diane came into my office and said, with real excitement in her voice, "You know, we actually have enough money coming in this month to pay the bills. And we'll even have some left over."

We'd been in business for 8 months.

What I knew, that she didn't, was that there was more coming where that had come from. With the way I was taking on new clients, we had gone way beyond the days of worrying if that initial $50,000 would hold out. We would finish our first year comfortably in the black—even though there had been a lot of days when it didn't look like that would ever happen—and that there was what looked like unlimited opportunity and a prosperous future out there ahead of us.

We had made it.

That was one of the happiest days of my life so, almost immediately, I came down off what had been about and 8 month high—a hypo manic state that never came close to the psychotic proportions of my previous episode but that had been real, nonetheless. I had been able to work long hours without sleep and to do the work of two people. My mind was fertile with ideas and I had all the energy I needed to return calls, travel, make pitches to new clients, and do whatever else needed to be done to make my infant business grow and survive. It was almost as though my disease had given me a gift. A small peace offering for all the misery it had caused me earlier.

Now, with the need for it gone, I came down off that high and fell into a severe, but manageable depression.

So, success at last and I responded by becoming depressed, which is the standard bi-polar pattern. Think of it this way: What goes up, must come down.

But since I had not been on a psychotic high, the depression was not the immobilizing thing it had been before. It was there, certainly, and there was nothing good to be said about it except that it was … well, *manageable*.

I was able to get out of bed and go into the office and do an honest day's work. I did this because I had to. The business depended on it, which meant that other people depended on it. They depended on *me*.

So I had to fall back on the things I'd already learned, on the strategies I'd developed for getting something done on those days when, if you don't watch out and take charge of things, you will simply sit and stare at the wall. I used the techniques I'd picked up in those *Recovery Inc.* sessions. And from Dr. Low's book. "Move your muscles." "Endorse yourself." " "Helplessness is not hopelessness." And so on.

It worked. Because it *had* to work.

And this brings me back to where I started this chapter. With my being "lucky," especially in the people I know and have known. Clients, friends, both.

Among the worst elements of any mental disease—certainly of the one I suffer from—is a feeling of isolation and terrible loneliness. I suspect that for people like artists, who work alone and do not have daily working relationships and contacts, this feeling of loneliness can be insupportable and unbearable and lead someone to believe that the only way out is suicide. I believe this explains the sad end of so many artists, poets, and writers who were bi-polar.

I was lucky in that I dealt with people every day and had those friends and clients, like Robbie Shipp who, by the way, was never aware of my affliction during our entire professional relationship. He learned about it later, after I'd learned what it was called and was in treatment for it and no longer hiding it from the people around me.

Before that, I had to bluff. And I became very good at it. So good that people like Robbie had a hard time believing me, at first, when I told them about my problem.

"In all my years of dealing with Steve," he told someone a couple of months before I wrote this, "I never knew. Never suspected. Never saw any sign that I can remember. He was always just 'Steve.' Always up and always fun to be around. I was shocked when he told me and sometimes I still find it hard to believe."

It wasn't easy, bluffing this way. But as I think back on it, I have to say it was worth it. For one thing, even though people were becoming more enlightened in their attitudes about mental illness, it would have still been a risk for me to let people know. I would have lost clients and, who knows, maybe the business. I certainly believed that, back then, so that made it worth it to bluff and to "carry on," as the Brits say, even when I didn't feel like it.

But it was also worth it because to bluff my way through, I had to force myself to do those things every bi-polar patient must do when dealing with this condition. I had to force myself, in short, not to give in.

I don't want to come off sounding noble here, but it is true that a big part of my reason for bluffing and making myself do the things I had to do—for dealing with my affliction like it was an enemy and I was in a fight—was that I would have been letting other people down if I hadn't. Responsibility was a burden, in one sense. But it was also a gift in another.

Two of my heroes from history are Abraham Lincoln and Winston Churchill. Both were bi-polar. Both learned how to deal with it and both, certainly, did great things. I would never compare myself to those two giants. That would be absurd. But in my own way, I found the strength to do what I had to do the same way they did. Lincoln couldn't give in and give up; his problems and agonies were too small when measured against his responsibilities. The ordeal of the nation in a Civil War dwarfed his emotional terrors. Churchill suffered from what he called his "black dog," and you read about it in the biographies. But resisting Hitler and the Blitz and the other awesome responsibilities and pressures Churchill faced as Prime Minister made his own dark spells almost insignificant. He couldn't give in … so he didn't. The word that describes him best may be "resolute." As a leader, certainly, and also as a bi-polar sufferer.

Me? I merely had a business to run. Still, in one sense, the comparison is not overdone. I always felt that something larger and more important than me and my struggles was at stake. Diane depended on me. And Robbie. And then more and more clients and more and more employees.

I'm grateful to all of them.

Like I said earlier. I've been very lucky.

Especially when it comes to people.

CHAPTER 22

CHAPTER 22

Now what? What do you do once you have learned that your start-up will, in fact, survive?

What was my next move after Diane walked into my office to tell me that enough money had come in from clients that we could afford to pay our bills and still have cash left over?

Well, the answer is both simple and complicated.

The simple part of the answer is: You make the business grow.

The complicated part is: How?

For 20 years, until I sold to my employees, I worked hard to make my business more profitable. Like just about every entrepreneur, I suspect, I thought about this almost every day and some days, I thought about nothing else. And in my case, it paid off. To put it plainly, I was successful and I got rich.

I was successful in spite of all the roadblocks that are out there and that every entrepreneur must navigate around. And I was successful, also, in dealing with my own, private affliction. I'll talk about that part, at length, in the next chapter. For now, though, let's stick to business.

What was, you might ask, the "secret of your success?"

Well, to give you an honest answer ... I don't really know.

If there is a "secret" to success—mine or anyone else's—then it is *still* a secret. At least to me. If there were a secret and I were in on it, then I would make a fortune by selling it to would-be entrepreneurs who would use it to guarantee their own success.

Still, I have been asked, many times, how to start a business and make it grow and become successful. It is one of the great American preoccupations.

Many, many people want to think of themselves as entrepreneurs-in-waiting and I've talked to a lot of them, sometimes in formal situations, like in panel discussions, and sometimes casually, like at cocktail parties.

One thing I've told everyone is that if you're thinking about starting a business, you should go one of two ways: either find a niche—come up with an original idea—or go with something where you already have the skills and expertise and can use them to build your business.

Obviously, it is hard to come up with a completely new idea. But if you are, say, Fred Smith and you have an idea for a way of delivering mail overnight, then your company becomes FedEx and you have one the great business success stories on your hands. In the world of catalog marketing, back when I started my business, there were a lot of people finding little niche markets that they could fill. You had catalogs for just about every imaginable interest and some of them became quite successful.

Someone came up with a catalog that handled patio furniture. It was pretty successful, as I remember. But nothing like, say, a little outfit that started out doing sexy lingerie and selling it through a racy catalog. *Victoria's Secret*, of course, became a huge success based on that original idea for serving a niche market. It was never a client—a little *too* racy, in my estimation. We were afraid that if we took that account on, it might chase other clients off. But *Banana Republic* was a client. The niche idea here was to appeal to wanderlust in people. The first catalogs featured safari jackets, panama hats, passport wallets, photographer's vests and other products that suggested kind of 1930's and 40's world of Hemingway and international glamour. The company grew and grew, of course. I helped it grow. Now it is a huge retailer selling khakis and t-shirts and the rest. But it started as a little niche catalog operation.

People came up with all sorts of ideas for catalogs. Tennis apparel was one. Gourmet cheeses. Cigars. It was a wild, wide-open time in catalog sales.

I wasn't smart enough to think of an entirely original business so I had to take the other path. I went into something I already knew and was good at. The challenge, then, was to be better at it than my competitors.

Right away, that meant doing a couple of things. First, I made up my mind that I was going to be someone who was available to my clients who were, after all, my customers

I don't believe there is any one-size-fits-all secret to success in business, but there are guaranteed routes to failure and one the most common is to ignore your customers and their needs. When I was at Brookstone and still thinking about going off on my own, I heard stories of list brokers and consultants who were hard to reach on the phone and who never—or almost never—came by to visit their clients. One of my first prospects, after I'd started my new business, told me that he was doing business with several list brokers and never saw any of them. They did business by mail and phone. I'm not sure I could have done that even if I'd tried. It's just not in my nature. I *like* the give and take of interpersonal relations and I would never have been any good at my business if I'd stayed at arm's length from my clients. And, evidently, a lot of those clients felt the way I did about close, personal attention, because the prospect who told me he never saw any of the several list brokers he dealt with ... well, he fired them all and hired me.

One of my other objectives when I started my business was to be completely professional. That meant that when you signed up with Millard Inc., you would be dealing with people who had a strong background catalog marketing. Some of my competitors had a background in things like furniture sales and I felt like that had to show. My background was in marketing and when I started growing, I hired only people whose background was in marketing. We might be wrong, occasionally, but it wasn't because we were winging it.

Next, I made it a point to treat my people well and to pay them well. When I was big enough to hire consultants myself, and have them look at my business, they would say, "Your payroll costs are awfully high. Maybe you ought to cut them."

And I would say, "No. Not happening."

If they asked me to explain, I would say that I wanted the people who worked for me to feel like they were being treated fairly and compensated fairly. Those people were the reason I was successful and I owed them. Also, at a more practical level, I didn't want them out looking around for another job because they thought they were underpaid. For this reason, I had almost no turnover of key people in the twenty years I owned the business. Loyalty down breeds loyalty up.

As part of this strategy, none of my sales people worked on commission. They were always on salary and a good one. They made more, usually, than they would have if they *had* been working on commission. And this way, they were never tempted to push something on a client that the client didn't want. If one of my people was working with a client on testing some lists, I didn't want him getting the client to test ten lists when six would have been enough. (I'll explain how this works a little later.)

People liked working for Millard, Inc. (which later became The Millard Group) and I'll tell you a funny little story about that. Some years after I'd started the business, I went to an appointment with my doctor (my therapist, actually, because by now, I had at last been diagnosed as bi-polar and was getting professional help) and when the two of us had finished up, he walked with me through the reception room and out to the door. On the way back to his office, his receptionist said to him, "You know who that *was*. That was Steve Millard. He's the best boss I ever had."

My therapist and I have laughed about that, many times.

"You must have been an awfully good boss," he said, "for her to say that about you to her *current* boss."

"Well," I said, "I tried."

And, in truth, I did. I did small things to let my employees know that I was grateful for their good work. For instance, every Monday morning I had fresh flowers bought in and put on the desks of all the women who worked in the office. I suspect that I was sensitive to this sort of thing because I accomplished my own startup fairly late in life and had a lot of experience down lower on the food chain. I remembered those days down in Texas, driving those lonesome highways and racking those supermarkets, so I felt a sense of empathy with the people who were working for me. I understood, I think, how much a show of support and loyalty from the top could mean.

For instance, we were up and running but still not so big and successful that we could afford to pass up business, when I started having trouble with one of our clients. Actually, *I* wasn't the one having the problem. It was my employees.

We had this client—actually, it was our second largest account at the time— and the boss of the outfit was a young, arrogant kid who had been handed the reins by his parents. He hadn't really worked to get where he was. As the old saying goes, he was born on third base, thinking he'd hit a triple.

So he had no feeling or consideration for anyone who hadn't been as lucky as he'd been. He thought he was the smartest guy in any room and he went out of his way to make sure everyone knew it.

He was also a bully and one of the things he did to make himself feel superior was call up my office and talk to my people in an abusive way. He'd use all sorts of foul language and tell my people how dumb they were. That sort of thing. He reduced some of the women in my office to tears and I'm sure that was exactly his intention.

Well, the first time it happened, I called him up and I told him, as calmly as I could manage, that if he had a problem I'd appreciate it if he didn't take it out on my employees but would come straight to me and we'd get it sorted out. I wasn't going to fall to pieces when some little prima donna rich kid screamed at me over the phone. I'd been through a lot worse then that.

Well, he said, "okay," in a sullen sort of way. But before long, he was back at it with my employees and when I heard about it, I decided I wasn't going to put up with it any longer.

So I called him up and I said, "Listen you son-of-a-bitch, I told you about calling up my people and abusing them."

"So," he said.

"So, you're fired."

"You can't fire me. I'm the client."

"Well I just did it."

I hung up the phone and when I walked out into the big open part of the office, everyone stood up and applauded. It was embarrassing but it felt good, too.

The client tried to call back, but I didn't take his calls. I'd fired him and that was that. Diane said, "Are you sure? That's an awfully big account."

"Not big enough to put up with that kind of stuff. Anyway, don't worry. We'll get other, bigger accounts."

And we did. Lots bigger. And that outfit went under. The kid didn't know how to run a business.

So, those are some of the things that I believe contributed to my success. I had a reputation for integrity—I never made side deals where I would give discounts when were trying to land an account. At one time, that sort of thing was common in our industry but it always came back to bite you. One of your good clients, who was paying full freight, would find out you were offering discounts to other people for the same service and you'd lose a better account than the one you gained.

We had a reputation for integrity at Millard Group and I'm very proud of that. It meant a lot to me—still does—when the magazine *Direct,* which was the journal for our industry, did a "Hall of Frame' feature and included me as one of the "25 people who changed the catalog business," the citation included this line:

"Many feel that Steve upped the standards of the frequently maligned list industry. For sure, he was the leader in both bringing user-side marketing knowledge to us and specializing in catalogs."

"Upped the standards." I like that. I like that very much.

One more important thing I learned about building a successful business— and it probably seems so obvious as to be self-evident—is that you need to be sure about what, exactly, your business *is.* You may think you know what you are in business to do but as things move along, newer and larger opportunities may show themselves and you need to be alert to them. Be flexible and adaptable and trust your instincts.

When I was thinking about going out on my own, the picture in my mind was "Steve Millard, Consultant." I would go in and study my client's business and look for ways to help him make more money. That's what I'd done with Robbie

Shipp by persuading him to make his albums available with luxury bindings. Robbie paid me $1,000 a day, one day a month for my services. It was nice money for me and he got a very good return, given the success of those albums.

But at $1,000 a month, I was never going to become much more than a small businessman who was making it. There are only so many days, after all, and every client would expect to get full value for his money. I could spread myself only so thin and still do a good job. There were practical and ethical limits. I could succeed purely as a consultant—I was sure of that—but it might not be worth the effort given the expense of travel and running the office. I'd be better off working for someone else and pulling down a salary.

But there was a second element to what I was doing for Robbie.

I was his list broker. And it was as a list broker that I built my business

What, you might ask, is a list broker and what does one do?

Good questions and ones that I've been asked a lot. I still get asked those questions, though not as often as when I was in the business. And the best way I've come up with to answer is to say, "Think of me as being like a stock broker." A good stock broker does his research and makes his recommendations based on what he knows about your needs and your resources and various things about you that he has learned from building a relationship. He knows about your tolerance for risk, for instance. He makes his recommendations and decisions based on these things and he is paid a commission on the trades he makes for your account.

There are some brokers, of course, who will make a lot of trades because it means more commissions for them. So they are putting their interests ahead of yours. That gets back to the integrity issue I was talking about earlier.

In the catalog industry, everyone is working off mailing lists. You build your business by adding names to your list. One way to do this is to pay another company for the use of its list. You "rent" the list and send out a catalog to every name on it. This is a one-time thing. But when someone orders something from one of those catalogs, the company renting the list now has the name which goes on *its* lists. If a good percentage of the people getting your catalog actually send in orders, then you may rent the list again. And again. If not, then you'll look for other lists to rent.

When I explain this to people, they usually say, "So that's the reason I keep getting those catalogs I never asked for?"

"Yep," I'll say. "You can blame me for that."

Then, one of the questions that always seems to come up is, "How do you keep someone from using the list more than once?" They have the names, after all, so why wouldn't they just keep using them over and over without paying the original owner of the list a fee?

Well, we had a technique for preventing that. It's one of the tricks of the trade. Whenever I rented a list for a client, I would stick a dummy name in among the real ones. I used the name of my cat and my home address. If I got one catalog from the company renting the list, that was all right. It was supposed to happen. If I got a *second* catalog, then I knew the company that had rented the list was bootlegging it—using it again without paying for it. Because my cat certainly wasn't ordering anything.

Occasionally, I'd catch a company doing this. When it happened, word got around and pretty soon, nobody would rent to that outfit. That was like a death sentence.

So, getting back to the business of being a list broker. What, you might ask, made someone—me, for example—better at it than someone else—my competitors, for instance?

Knowledge. Experience. Hard work. All the usual things. I made sure I understood the businesses I was renting from and renting for. That's critical. I could study a business so that I'd know where to find lists that would appeal to its customers. And I began developing ways of segmenting lists so that you'd rent, say, only people who had made an order of over $100 in the last 90 days. Or people from certain zip codes. Or only women. There are all kinds of ways you can segment a list. And the idea is always to find the best return. The company that owns the list rents at a certain price per name so you can save the client money by renting fewer names but picking the right ones so that he gets a higher percentage of orders.

This is where a reputation for integrity comes in, again. You are being paid a commission out of that rental fee so if you didn't have your client's interest in mind and just wanted the highest possible commission and the fastest possible buck, you could have him renting lots of lists and you wouldn't try to cherry pick the best names from a list.

I didn't do that and people knew I didn't do that. And that reputation was one of the most important factors in the growth and success of my business.

It started with Robbie when I told him that I would still do the consulting for him and I would do it for free. In exchange, I wanted to do list brokerage for him, at the standard commission, which was 10 percent.

I would look for other operations with customers that might be likely to buy what Robbie was selling and I would rent their lists for him and test them and if they worked, his business would grow rapidly, if not exponentially. The success would be measurable and verifiable, which is not always the case with consulting success where your suggestions might be good even when the return on them isn't immediately evident on the bottom line.

Robbie agreed to my proposition. Eagerly, in fact. And I figured that if I made the handling of lists my business with all my clients, and I succeeded at it, then I would grow a lot faster than if I were doing consulting and periodically raising my fee.

So, not long after that "good news" meeting I had with Diane, I got a call from Leigh Perkins of Orvis, the man who had once offered me a job at a salary that was considerably lower than what I'd been making at the time and told me that I should be happy with the offer since it included the "geographic compensation" of living in Manchester, Vermont.

I'd turned Leigh down, of course, but I kind of hated to do it since I liked him and because his business, which was fly-fishing, was also my passion. But there were no hard feelings. Like a lot of other people in the direct mail business, Leigh called after I'd been on my own for a while and was building a reputation.

"I hear you've become the catalog guru since we last talked," he said. "That's what people say, anyway."

"Well," I said, "who am I to argue."

Lee laughed. He is a big laugher.

"Well, I'm not sure I can afford you."

"You couldn't the last time we talked," I said.

He laughed at that, too.

Then he said, "Well, come on over. I'll pay your rate. We need help"

So I drove over from New Hampshire and had lunch with Leigh and some of his key people. After hearing what they had to say, I made them what was now my usual deal. I told them I would be happy to look at the business and function as a consultant and that I wouldn't charge them a fee for doing it. What I wanted, in return, was to be their exclusive list broker. I'd learned, in my conversations with them, that they were dealing with several list brokers. None of them were very close by and, according to Leigh, he and his people had "never even met them."

He agreed to my deal. I became Orvis' exclusive list broker and they got the benefit of my consulting services at no charge.

It was a real win-win.

I took my consulting duties seriously and came up with several ideas that made Leigh money. I told him to stop wasting money by putting pre-stamped envelopes in his catalogs. He resisted at first. I think because he believed it was somehow undignified of Orvis to ask its high-quality customers to buy and lick stamps. But I was right and I saved him several thousand dollars. He appreciated the advice. Especially since it didn't cost him anything.

Meanwhile, I was handling the list business for him and making far more in commissions than I would have ever made as a consultant at $1000 a day. So I'd become a list broker who threw in some consulting as an extra. It made sense for me to spend a little time under the hood of my clients' businesses. I needed to understand what they did and a little about how they did it if I wanted to come up with the right lists for them to use. The clients appreciated my interest and they especially appreciated it if I could help them out in my role as a consultant. That made them loyal to me and I had competitors who would have been only too happy to come in an underbid me or find some other way to separate me from my clients. But clients didn't leave me. And I'm sure part of the reason is that they believed I understood their business and cared about it more than if I had been strictly a list broker and done business at arm's length.

There was something else, too. Something that wasn't strictly about business. If I'd been a paid consultant, the demands on my time would have been very heavy. Perhaps even too heavy for me to handle. When you fly in somewhere to work with someone as his consultant, your day does not run from nine to five. People expect you to go out for a drink after the close of business and then to join them for dinner someplace. And if they are paying you, it is just about impossible to say "no."

But there were plenty of days when I needed to say, "no." Those would be the days when I was in one of my depressions and when it was all I could do to get out of bed and make a scheduled call to visit with a client.

I knew I could do that. And I knew I could bluff my way through the day. By now, I'd had plenty of experience with bluffing. But by the end of the day, I needed to get away and be alone and if I wasn't being paid as a consultant, it was easy to come up with an excuse and an apology.

On days like that, I would feel this tremendous, almost desperate, need to be alone and it was always a relief to get back to my room and sit there with a drink. Or two.

I wouldn't describe my drinking, then or now, as "heavy." But I certainly wasn't an occasional "social" drinker, either. My drinking was a way of "self-medicating." I realize that and I don't advise it. But the fact is that I drank because it helped me deal with this nameless thing that came and went and that could, on bad days, make my life a living hell.

My drinking, back then, helped me get through some very tough days. I didn't have any professional help and I didn't have any medication. I had those methods of dealing with my problem that I had developed on my own and through the *Recovery, Inc.* meetings and through reading—and rereading—Dr. Low's book.

And ... I had whiskey.

When I think about those days and my relationship with alcohol, I'm reminded of a story I once read about the comedian, George Gobel, who was very popular back in the 1950's. Gobel was backstage, one evening, waiting to go on and there was a much younger entertainer, one of the other acts, standing there with him. While they were waiting, Gobel was taking an occasional sip from a pint bottle of Four Roses whiskey.

The younger entertainer watched this and finally said, in a tone of disapproval, "Mr. Gobel, do you always drink whiskey before you go on stage?"

Gobel looked at him and said, "Yes. Don't you?"

"Certainly not."

"You mean to tell me," Gobel said, "that you go out there *all alone?*"

I'm not sure I could have made it all alone, back in those days. Drinking never caused me to miss a day of work and, in fact, it was probably the other way around. Knowing that the day would eventually end and I could sit down alone with a bourbon old-fashioned made it possible for me to get through a lot of days I might not have otherwise been able to handle.

I don't recommend using alcohol. But I haven't quit drinking, either. That old-fashioned at the end of the day is still something I look forward to and that I enjoy intensely.

CHAPTER 23

Those early years, when I was building the business, seemed to go by awfully fast. I was working long hours and traveling a lot. There was a certain amount of stress and sometimes … there was a lot of stress. There is no getting around it—if you want to go out on your own, then you have to be prepared to deal with the pressure because, ultimately, everything comes back to you, everyone depends on you, and all the problems are your problems. It is a lot easier when you are working for someone else and letting that person take the responsibility. After I went out on my own, I was that person.

I've had people ask me—especially if they knew about my struggles with bi-polar disease—if the hard work and the stress wasn't too much. Or if it was worth it.

The answers are: no and yes.

It is true that I had to deal with some extra difficulties that came with my being bi-polar. There were days—and plenty of them—when I *really* didn't want to go into the office. It wasn't just the kind of normal reluctance that everyone feels now and then when you are overworked or just tired of what you are doing and ready for a break. I was in the kind of state that I've described earlier where it was a big damned accomplishment to get out of bed and into the shower. To get dressed and feed the dogs. But I always did it and I always went into work. I just made myself do it.

And that, as I've said earlier, is something I might not have been able to do if I had *not* been the boss; if it hadn't been my business and people hadn't been depending on me. In that way, I think having responsibility makes dealing with bi-polar disease ... well, not *easier* in the ordinary sense of that word, but more manageable. Earlier, I used the examples of Lincoln and Churchill who were both bi-polar and had wars to run and those wars weren't going to take time-out until the President or Prime Minister felt better and was ready to take charge again. Me, I was merely running a list brokering business out of New Hampshire and the larger world would not have noticed or cared if it failed because the boss kept missing work. But I felt intensely responsible for that business and the people who worked there and that feeling was something that pushed me to do what I needed to do in spite of my depression or anxiety or other symptoms of my bi polar condition.

And, then, there was the whole business of bluffing my way through. Keeping that kind of secret is hard work. You are on the alert all the time; afraid to let down your guard. That just added to the stress of running the business.

So, sometimes, the pressure got to me a little. As for whether or not it was worth is, I've already said that my answer is "yes."

That's wrong. The correct answer is "*hell, yes.*"

One of the main reasons I wanted to write this book is that, on looking back, I realize what a wonderful time I've had and how lucky I've been. I may be bi-polar and some people might look at that and say I was dealt a bad hand. Some days, I think that myself.

But then I look at all that I've accomplished, all the friends I've made, all the fun I've had ... I look at that I think, "Well, I fought through it and it didn't keep me down. I've got no complaints."

I mean that. Starting the business and then building it and making it into a success may have been stressful from time to time but it was also a lot of fun. There may have been some bad days—and also some *really* bad days—but there were many, many more days when I felt like it would have been impossible for anyone to enjoy life any more than I did. When I not only didn't know what to call this mysterious intruder into my life, but when I didn't think about my condition at all. When I was symptom-free and just happy to be alive.

And one of the reasons that I felt that way is—life is better at the top. There may be stress in having responsibility and making decisions but there is also something very liberating about it. You aren't chained to someone else's desk, having to make things work according to his way of thinking which you might think is totally wrong.

I had my disagreements with my staff and if my mind wasn't changed after I'd listened to their arguments what I would say is this: "Okay. Now be reasonable. Do it *my* way."

And they did, because they didn't have any choice.

There is a lot to be said for having the final say.

Another reason that I was able to enjoy life as the boss so much is that I got to deal with other people who had started their own businesses, like I had. Most of them were my kind of people. We spoke the same language and we dealt with the same kind of challenges. Many of them were more like colleagues than clients. Some of them became close, lifelong friends.

I've already mentioned Robbie Shipp who was my first client and is one of those lifelong friends. There was another, a man named Gary Comer who was the founder of Lands' End.

Gary called me not long after I went out on my own. He told me he was working in advertising out in Chicago but he had this catalog business that he was building. It had started out selling nautical stuff to people who liked to sail—which explained the name—and he was thinking of moving out into soft goods. But he needed help if he was going to do it, he said, and he'd heard that I was the person who could help him. Would I be interested?

Well, like I said, I wasn't turning down any work at the point. I had three clients, at that time, and I needed a lot more than that. So I said I would be glad to come out to Chicago and talk but there was one thing I had to do first.

One of those three clients was a little gift catalog outfit on the other side of New Hampshire and it had a kind of sailing theme. I thought I ought to check and make sure that client wouldn't object if I took on Lands' End. It seemed like the ethical thing to do.

Sure enough, that client *did* object and I had to call Gary back and explain that I couldn't go to work for him. I said I was sorry and he said, "Call me if things change."

And they did.

A few months after that conversation, the client on the other side of the state stopped paying his bills. Gary had sounded like he would at least be a paying client so I called him back. A couple of days later, I was on my way to Chicago where he put me up in the Drake Hotel, right on the lake front on the very toney near-north side of town.

Gary's two little girls were in the car with him when he picked me up. He dropped the girls off at school and we went to his office on West Madison. The office was a mess and one of the things adding to the clutter was a stack of mail from people offering to rent him their mailing lists.

"I don't know which to use," he said, "or how much to pay ... or anything about handling lists. That's what I need your help doing."

I told him he had come to the right place and we went to work. We had to sit on the floor of the office to go through all the correspondence and pick which lists to follow up on and which to throw away. When we'd finished, we'd made a very good start and I had one of my very best clients.

From them on, when I needed to meet with Gary, I would fly out to Midway Airport in Chicago and he would meet me there in his little Cessna. We'd take off and fly across the lake to Dodgeville, Wisconsin where he'd built this huge new building. He'd fly in low and buzz the building. He said he did it, "To warn them that the boss is coming." Then, we'd land on this little short airstrip where it seemed to me we just barely cleared some phone wires as were coming in on final. Once we were there, we'd work all day and it almost wasn't like work since he was such a cheerful, easy-going guy. We had a wonderful relationship.

Of course, his business grew like crazy. He had a great sense of what people wanted in the way of casual and traditional clothes and how to make them affordable. His stuff was good but inexpensive and it caught on. In the space of just a few years, he went from $5 million in sales to $15 million in profits. Sears eventually bought the business.

For $1.4 *billion*.

Lands' End was one of my biggest and most important clients but that didn't keep one of their competitors from calling me. I'd known Leon Gorman of L.L. Bean since he'd called me for advice while I was still at Brookstone. We'd remained friendly and Leon had had me up to Maine to fish with him at his club. But he wasn't a client. He was with the man down in Texas, the one I'd talked with before I went out on my own and had turned down when he offered to go partners.

A couple of years after I started with Gary at Lands' End, I got a call from Leon. He wasn't happy with my competitor in Texas. He wanted to talk to me about becoming a client.

L.L. Bean would be a great account. It was one of the iconic brands in the entire catalog world. Just about everyone had heard of L.L. Bean of Freeport,

Maine and its 24 hour service and its signature boots with the lifetime guarantee. Having that name on my client list would be very, very good for the company.

But there was the small matter of Lands' End and Gary Comer. I didn't want to lose him as a client or a friend by taking on a competitor. I would have to talk to him and do a real selling job.

So, I talked to him and, of course, he said, "No." He just couldn't see how I could work for both companies. I said I understood and I called Leon who was almost as disappointed as I was.

I *knew* I could work for both companies as a list broker and do good job for both. It would be up to me, as an ethical professional, not to get into the business side of either company in a way that would give one an advantage over the other. As a list broker, my job would be to help them both grow their lists and I was sure I could do it so that there was no conflict of interest. I was convinced that I could, indeed, serve two masters.

So I wrote Gary a letter. I have never worked harder on a letter to anyone in my life. I spent two days on it, explaining to Gary how much it would mean to my business to have Bean as a client and assuring him that I could ethically work for both of them. He knew my reputation, I said, and he knew he could trust me.

I wish I had kept a copy of that letter. I don't remember exactly what I said but it worked. Gary gave in and I took on Bean as a client. The reputation I'd built in the business paid off, once again. My commitment to doing things in an ethical way hadn't been a business decision. Not strictly, anyway. It just seemed like the way to go, for its own sake. But it proved to be good for business, too.

Very good, in fact.

There is a funny postscript to that story. Not too long after I'd gone to work for Leon, I went to his office to talk about something. Those days, I carried my papers and files and other work in one of those canvas briefcases that Lands' End sold by the millions and monogrammed with the customer's initials. I always used it and didn't think about it when I was packing to go to Freeport.

Well, I sat down in Leon's office and as we were making small talk before we got down to business, I had this sense that something was making him nervous. He kept looking away from me, toward something near the door. It didn't occur to me at the time but that was where I'd put my briefcase.

Finally, Leon got up and said, "Excuse me, I'll be right back."

He left the office and came back a few minutes later with one of those boat bags that Bean sold by the millions and was embroidered with the company name. He put the Land's End briefcase inside the L.L. Bean bag, then went around his desk, sat down, and said, "Now, where were we?"

He might not have had a problem with my carrying Lands' End as a client but he didn't want me carrying my stuff in one of there briefcases. There were some lines he would not cross.

I got back at him later, when Eddie Bauer—my client and his competitor— made a deal with Ford to sell a line of SUVs that carried the Eddie Bauer logo. I had one and I drove it up to Freeport for one of my meetings with Leon. Before I went out to see him, I carefully cut out the L.L. Bean logo from a catalog and taped it over the Eddie Bauer logo.

When I saw Leon, I said, "This wagon of yours is wonderful, Leon. A real pleasure to drive. Wonder why Eddie Bauer didn't think to do it."

He took it gracefully.

Leon was a good fishing companion and so was Leigh Perkins of Orvis. Leigh also introduced me to wingshooting. I'd never been a hunter before I stated handling Orvis as a client and got to be very good friends with Leigh. He kept telling me how much he enjoyed bird hunting and that I ought to try it. I kept saying I wasn't interested until, finally, he persuaded me to go, as his guest, to the shooting school that Orvis ran not far from the company headquarters in Manchester, Vermont.

I would have been ungracious not to go and I valued Leigh both as a client and a friend. I wasn't excited about the idea of shooting birds—even the clay kind—with a shotgun but by the end of the two-day school I was hooked. I began traveling the world for wingshooting. Scotland for driven grouse is something I dream about and one of my favorite photographs shows me with the six birds I killed with five shots. I also love Argentina for the dove and the ducks. I've hunted quail with Leigh at his plantation on the Florida/Georgia line. And I still go out to North Dakota for pheasant every fall with some old buddies.

I count learning about wingshooting—which became one of my great loves, along with fly-fishing—as one of the surprise benefits of starting my own business. But maybe the greatest emotional payoff took the form of a single business meeting.

After my company was up and established and a leader in the industry, I got a call from a possible client who wanted me to visit headquarters and meet with top management.

It had been a long time since I'd had any dealings with the *Reader's Digest*. The last time I had been inside the company's headquarters in Chappaqua, I'd been escorted to the door. Banished as a crazy man. Which, in fact, I was.

Now, years later, the company was floundering and turning to me, of all people, for help.

I made the trip and the meeting. There was no way I was going to turn down the opportunity to go back inside that building. It was a strange experience, walking through those doors. I felt some nervousness, at first, but that passed and in its place there was this feeling of enormous gratitude. I felt so fortunate to have come back so far. There was no sense of vindication or anything like that.

The *Digest* certainly hadn't treated me unfairly. I had been blessed by fortune with friends and opportunities and now I could look back on that other time and feel like it truly was behind me.

I wish I could say that the meeting was a big success and that after it was over I took on the *Digest* as a client and reversed its sagging fortunes. But it didn't happen that way and I knew it wouldn't when I walked into a conference room and saw more than a dozen people seated around a table.

You don't get things done with committees of that size. Predictably, nothing came of the meeting and the slow decline of the *Digest* continued.

Still … it was a day I'll never forget. I had been asked to help bail out the *Digest*. The last time I'd left that building, it was under escort and virtually in restraints. I felt an old and painful sense of disgrace lifted off of me and I thank God for letting me live to experience it.

Success may never have tasted sweeter than it did, for me, that day.

CHAPTER 24

CHAPTER 24

S o I was successful in business and had managed to bring myself back professionally so thoroughly that even the *Reader's Digest* was coming to me for help. But I was not "cured" and I never would be. I didn't know this as a matter of science but I'm sure I was beginning to grasp it in an intuitive way. Whatever my affliction was called, it was my burden to bear and I continued doing the things that had been working for me since those dark days in Nyack when I had turned to wood carving as a way to "move my muscles," and attended those *Recovery Inc.* sessions where I learned the other techniques that Dr. Low advocated as a way of dealing with problems like mine.

I was still "toughing it out" and "faking it." And none of the people who worked for me knew of my problem. Nor did any of my clients including those like Robbie Shipp, Leigh Perkins, and Leon Gorman who became friends and with whom I spent a great deal of time away from business. My secret was still my secret and I believed I could keep it that way. I had some difficult times—with anxiety and depression, especially—but I managed to keep the lid on tight.

Then, six or seven years after I'd started the business, I hit a very bad patch. The "trigger," to use Dr. Low's phrase was, once again, intimacy. I had become involved with a woman and asked her to marry me and the prospect sent me over the edge, just as it had on three previous occasions.

Some people never learn.

I was in such a bad way that it was impossible to keep it from the people who worked closely with me. They saw the extreme agitation and distractibility. They saw me lose control in ways they had never seen before. Saw me irrationally angry over little things and paying obsessive attention to small details. I cry easily, anyway, and they saw me weep without much provocation.

They cared about me and they were worried and they decided they had to do something. One of them had been seeing a psychotherapist in town and had a very high opinion of the man. One of my key people asked if he could speak to me, in private, and when I said, "Yes," he said, "Steve, you need help. There's somebody you should talk to."

It is a measure of my distress that I agreed I needed help. It had been a years since I'd seen anyone "professionally" about my problems. I'd given up on that, I thought, a long time ago.

But now, here I was.

I called and made an appointment with the man who changed my life: Dr. Gerald Kraines.

Gerry is a Harvard-trained clinical psychiatrist and one of the most brilliant men I have ever known. And he not exclusively a medical man. He has a restless streak. Gerry worked on public health projects in Central America in the rural parts of this country. He is also an entrepreneur. He founded the first mental health HMO in New Hampshire and a few years after I started seeing him, he left the world of medicine and became CEO of the Levinson Institute which works with businesses, consulting on organization and leadership. He wrote a book on the subject, called *Accountability Leadership*, that is very highly regarded.

I bring this up to make an important point—namely that Gerry and I are very much alike and approach life in similar fashion. When I went to see him, I was not dealing with a remote, cold, professional figure who put me off immediately so that the relationship became formal and almost antagonistic. That is what had happened, often, in the past and was why it had been so long since I had sought professional help.

With Gerry, it was different. I liked him right away. And trusted him almost that quickly.

I want to pause in the telling of my story, just for a moment, to make an important point: There are many, many professionals out there who have the training to help people with problems like mine. But they are not perfect copies of each other. They are people and no two people are entirely alike. If you need help and you go to a professional and are not satisfied with the relationship or the treatment ... then *change doctors*. And keep on changing doctors until you are seeing someone you are comfortable with. Nothing is more important that this.

Okay, back to my story.

I was skeptical but desperate the first time I went to see Gerry. I doubted very much that he could help me but I was willing to try anything. Right away, I liked his face and his manner. Something warm and friendly showed through the professional mask and he was plainly and genuinely interested in me and concerned about my problems. I was experienced enough at bluffing and faking to know it when I saw it and I didn't see it in Gerry.

So I answered freely and honestly when he started asking questions. We went through my entire history and I laid it all out for him. From the first episode in Hawaii, through the psychotic breakdown in Chappaqua, and the extended period of depression in Nyack, right up to my present agonies

He listened and he asked questions and then he made his diagnosis.

I was bi-polar.

I'm sure it wasn't the first time I'd heard the term. But I was so far into denial that had stopped thinking about what to call my condition or even, really, to be very curious about it. I knew it only as my secret and something I had to deal with and the less I thought about it—or even knew about it—the better.

But now, at long last, it had a name.

"Bi-polar?" I said. "Not schizophrenia?"

"No. That was a clear mis-diagnosis. Were you ever diagnosed as having unipolar depression?"

"No. I don't think so, anyway."

"That's the most common misdiagnosis. Patients who are actually bi-polar are often treated for depression."

"There's a difference?" It was an honest question. To me, it was all just "the problem" and it didn't make much difference what you called it.

"Yes," Gerry said. "There is a difference. Quite a bit. Both in symptoms and in treatment."

"Then this ... this bi-polar thing *can* be treated?"

"Yes," Gerry said. "It can."

And that was the beginning of a new phase of my life.

As you can imagine, I was eager to get started on the treatment that Gerry said was possible. After all these years, I couldn't wait. I was only slightly less eager to learn what I could about this condition that, at last, had a name. Bi-polar.

What was it and what did it mean to suffer from it? What caused it? What, if anything, cured it and why did I have it.

My questions were basic, almost childish, but I wanted answers so I read as much as I could about bi-polar disorder and I asked Gerry many, many questions, which he answered with infinite patience.

I can't imagine anyone who, upon being diagnosed as bi-polar, wouldn't do the same. Knowledge is sunlight and the more you know, the less you fear. The less you fear, the stronger you are. And the stronger you are, the better you are able to fight back against this intruder in your life.

And believe me, it will be a fight. One that never ends.

The literature on bi-polar disorder is extensive. If you suffer from the condition, or a member of your family does, then I strongly recommend that you consult the books and learn what you can. I am not a medical professional—far from it—so I will not try to make this book into a short course on bi-polar disorder. I will suggest books. And I will site some of the things I have learned from my own reading, which has been going on for almost 50 years now. These are things that strike me as especially interesting and especially useful if you are in this long, lifetime fight with your own intruder.

Bi-polar disorder, is what it sounds like and what an earlier term—*manic-depressive*—may have described more accurately. My wild psychotic state during my last months at the *Digest* and my profound, immobilizing depression during the two years I was in Nyack are both manifestations of the condition. Put simply, you go up and come down. If you are bi-polar, you can't experience one without the other.

Sometimes you go so far up you completely lose touch with reality, as I had when I'd thought of myself as the "Redeemer" and was expecting visits from Abraham Lincoln. This is called a "manic" phase. Sometimes you are high but still tethered to reality, as I had been for the 8 months after I had gone out on my own and it was touch- and-go as to whether or not my new business would succeed. This is called "hypo-mania" and in some circumstances, since it makes you more energetic and creative, it can be your friend.

Until, that is, you crash. Which always happens. What goes up, must come down. When you are down, you are in a state of depression and it can be crippling and so profound that you will consider suicide as a means of escape as I had that night when I put the Lugar to my head.

There are other phases along the bi-polar spectrum. Periods when a patient is largely symptom-free; a condition called *euthymia*. Then, there can be periods where the symptoms of both mania and depression are present. These are called *mixed episodes*.

If you are bi-polar but never experience an episode of true mania, like my breakdown while I was still at the *Digest*, then you suffer from bi-polar disorder 2. Some patients swing wildly from one extreme to the other and this is called *rapid cycling*.

Bipolar disorder affects millions of Americans. Somewhere between 3 to 5 percent of the population. Fewer than 1/3 of these people are in treatment and of those who are not, 20 percent will attempt suicide. Among people who are diagnosed as bi-polar, the risk of suicide is 30 times greater than that of the general population.

Bi-polar disorder is, in short, very real, a very serious public health problem … and a killer.

Many historical figures suffered from bi-polar disorder, to include my heroes Churchill and Lincoln. Also a number of celebrated artists and writers. Both Hemingway and Faulkner were bi-polar.

As I learned more in my own studies, a great many things came back to me and began to make a certain kind of sense. I saw myself, for instance, in the mnemonic that is used to describe a manic episode. You remember the word DIGFAST and here is what each letter stands for:

Distractibility—loss of focus, excessive multi-tasking

Insomnia—long periods with no need for sleep

Grandiosity—inflated self-esteem

Flight of ideas—complaints of racing thoughts

Activity—increased goal directed activities

Speech—excessive talking. Garrulousness.

Thoughtlessness—risk-taking behavior. Sexual, financial, physical.

I could see myself in every one of those, especially as they applied to the crackup when I was at the *Digest*. The Redeemer ... the consultant with an office in New York and no clients ... the crazy affair ... the reckless driving ... the wild spending. And on and on. It was all there and it was all me. Or had been, anyway.

And, then, there was the mnemonic for a period of depression like the one that followed. The word to remember here is SIG-E-CAPS and it works out this way:

Sleep —insomnia and hypersomnia

Interest—loss of interest in normally pleasurable activities

Guilt—excessive and inappropriate feelings of guilt

Energy—excessive fatigue

Concentration—diminished ability to focus

Appetite—significant weight gain or loss

Psychomotor—agitation/retardation

Suicide—recurrent thoughts of death

Almost all of those were on the money as descriptions of me during that time in Nyack. It was strange and oddly liberating to recognize all those symptoms in my own experience. I was entirely persuaded by Gerry and by my own research that I was, indeed, bi-polar and had been, all along. I was one of the many, many bi-polar sufferers who either go undiagnosed or who are misdiagnosed, which can be just as serious. Treating bi-polar patients who are in a period of depression with drugs that work for someone who is unipolar depressive can dramatically worsen the symptoms.

But now, at long last, I had been diagnosed. I was in the care of a doctor who had recognized my illness and knew how to treat it. But there was this one problem—the treatment meant that I would be taking some kind of drug. And it was not just a one-time thing, either. Drug therapy meant taking the medicine regularly, routinely, and from now on.

I didn't like the sound of it.

Taking some kind of drug that way seemed like … well, like *weakness*. Like a kind of surrender. Once you started, you would be under the control of the drug, like some kind of zombie. It was a matter of pride, I suppose. I wanted to be in charge and if I went onto this medication, then the drug would be in the driver's seat and I would just be a passenger, along for the ride.

Gerry listened patiently to my objections and he seemed sincerely sympathetic to my resistance. As our discussions went on and I told him more about my history. I told him about the methods I come up with for coping and getting through the bad times and I told him about *Recovery Inc.* and about Dr. Low's book and how much it had helped me.

At some point in this conversation, Gerry smiled and said, "Yes. I've heard of Dr. Low. As a matter of fact, he and my father were colleagues in Chicago. He used to come to our house for dinner."

I've talked earlier about "signs" and how I had come to believe in them and take them seriously. I took this new information as a sign—if one were still needed—that I had the right doctor and that I should trust him and put myself into his care.

So we talked at length about Dr. Low and his techniques and how I helpful they had been for me. Gerry explained that this was now a recognized regime for treatment that even had its own name—cognitive therapy.

Gerry explained that cognitive therapy was, essentially, a program in which the patient used certain techniques, first to recognize the symptoms of the disease and, then, to get control over them or, at least, minimize them. It began, logically, with the patient recognizing that there was a problem and, then, deciding to take measures to deal with it. It depended on this. On the patient taking some initiative. It is tempting—even seductive—when you have a condition like mine to think of yourself as a victim and helpless.

If you decide—and it is a decision—to embark on a program of cognitive therapy—then you have decided that you will not be passive. This is the most important element. You may be ill but you are not helpless. You can fight.

That is the first and most important step ... recognizing that you are in a fight and you have resources. I'll get into this in the next chapter but for now, the important point is this: Gerry told me that I had been employing the cognitive therapy techniques ever since those dark days at Nyack. So much of what I'd told him about those days, he said, came right out of the cognitive therapy playbook. Which was not surprising since I had embraced, so thoroughly, the insights of Dr. Low.

"You know, Steve," Gerry told me, "I've seen a lot of bi-polar patients and none of them have shown the kind of determination and commitment you have. You are a poster child for cognitive therapy. I admire your discipline and your courage."

Coming from Gerry, that meant a lot. I was even a little embarrassed to hear him say it. I knew I had fought hard but I wasn't sure I'd always been fighting as hard as I could.

"You've succeeded," he said, "where many, many people have failed."

I told him I appreciated what he said. And I did. And I knew that I wasn't going to quit doing what I'd been doing for so many years now. It had worked and, by now, it was a habit.

"But you still think I should take this drug?"

"Yes."

"I don't know …"

"Why are you reluctant?"

"It sounds like I'm helpless."

"Spoken like someone who is good at cognitive therapy."

"You know what I mean. Like I need medication to function."

"Exactly. Listen, Steve, if you were diagnosed a being diabetic and I came to you with insulin, would you refuse it because you didn't want to have to depend on drugs?"

"No," I said. "I guess not."

"Well, for what you've got, this drug is just like insulin."

"What is it?"

"Lithium."

And he wrote me a prescription.

I was still reluctant. Not certain I would ever take it. But I got the prescription filled.

A night or two later, I was feeling that familiar blend of agitation and depression. That sense that things aren't right, something awful may be about to happen, and that you have no control and that maybe you don't want any. It is a hard feeling to describe and even harder to endure.

I had the medicine. But I hadn't taken it and had told myself I never would. That I would, one day, flush it down the toilet. But this night, I went into the bathroom and I opened the prescription bottle and held the pill in my hand.

And I thought, "Why not?" The worst would be better than a lot I had been through.

I took the pill.

It went down easily and in less than five minutes, I felt better. No, not just "better;" I felt *good*. Felt great. I felt this warmth and this feeling of well-being come over me like a soft blanket. The gloom seemed to dissolve and I was alert and alive.

It was a miracle. And that's how I described it to Gerry the next day.

He laughed.

"Placebo effect," he said. "There is no way, medically, that you could have gotten relief from those symptoms in such a short time. But I'm glad you took the medication and I want you to continue on it."

So I did. For 25 years, until new drugs came along and I switched from Lithium to Seroquel which has resulted in a dramatic improvement for my deep depressions.

At the time I started on Lithium, it had been available in the U.S. for about 15 years. It had been around a lot longer than that. It was used to treat gout in the early 19th century on the theory that excessive uric acid was the cause of gout and lithium crystals would dissolve uric acid crystals. In the course of their experiments, researchers decided to treat emotional problems with lithium since these were thought to be caused by an excess of uric acid.

This line of researched fizzled until the 1940s when, almost by accident, another researcher discovered that lithium tranquilized the rodents he was using in an experiment. One thing followed another and lithium became the first recognized drug for the treatment of mental illness. . Like so many things in life, the use of lithium for treatment of bi-polar disorder was a series of accidents. Nobody knew why it worked; only that it did.

It certainly worked for me, though after the first experience, Gerry and I both recognized that I was among that group of bi-polar patients for whom the drug was not especially effective in relieving the symptoms of depressions. It cut off the tops but did not put a hard floor on the bottoms. Also, lithium was to some degree a mood killer. Experiences that might have brought on euphoria in the past were now just pleasant. The drug quieted my emotions and modulated them.

For me, this was a great breakthrough, though I sometimes felt like I was living an excessively sedated life. But I knew, from hard experience, how bad things could get without the modulating effects of the drug. I took it religiously.

Which is not true of many bi-polar patients. As the widely used phrase has it, they "go off their meds." I suspect that many people who stop taking their medications—whatever they are—do so because they feel like they have gotten so much better that they don't need to take them any more. They feel, in short, like they are cured.

They are, of course, wrong. The medications do not "cure." They only control.

And, then, there are those patients who actually miss the old wild sensations of the hypo-manic stage of the disease when you are on top of things, full of energy and ideas, and all things seem possible. And this, of course, is understandable. Many, many people take drugs—or alcohol—to experience these same feelings, however fleetingly.

What I want to say to people who are reading these words and are on medication for bi-polar disorder—or any other psychiatric condition—is this:

Take your medication. Do not stop taking your medication. Keep taking your medication. Please.

I know it can be discouraging to be to feel dependent on medications. To feel medicated. To feel this sense that somehow your medications are cutting you off from the normal, exhilarating experiences of life.

But even when you feel this way—*especially* when you feel this way—you must keep taking your meds.

The most important single lesson I have come away with from a lifetime of dealing with what it took me a long time to learn was bi-polar disorder is this: You are in a never-ending struggle that requires, above everything else, discipline on your part if you are to hold your own. It took discipline for me to do the things

I had learned to do and that I later learned were part of a program of "cognitive therapy." It takes the same kind of discipline to keep taking your medications when you feel like you no longer want to or need to.

One major component of discipline is perseverance. You keep doing something, because you know you must, even when you can't see the payoff. Not even way off in the distance somewhere.

I persevered. That's the most, probably, that I'll give myself credit for, though Gerry Kraines might give me credit for more than that.

But perseverance yields big dividends. I'll give you a couple of quotes that sum up my feelings on the subject. The first is from the great basketball coach, John Wooten, who said:

"It's not so important who starts the game but who finishes it."

The other is from Churchill, who said:

"Success is not final, failure is not fatal: it is the courage to continue that counts."

I believe that if you continue, if you stay in the game, you will be rewarded. I know I was.

In the next chapter, I will try to explain, in a kind of handy, how-to form how I did it and how others might learn from my example.

CHAPTER 25

CHAPTER 25

In the last chapter, I promised to deal more fully with cognitive therapy and now it is time to do that. I need to say, again, what I have already said: I am not a medical doctor or an expert of any kind on the subject of bipolar disease. I am simply someone who has lived with it for 50 years. It has taken me to the very brink of suicide and it has caused me, in the 18 years when I was symptomatic, to suffer from depressions that sometimes seemed unendurable. In my struggles with this disease, I often felt like I was fighting a never-ending war.

If you were to think of this as a book about war, then, it might be helpful to consider it not as a something written by a general, strategist, or historian. It is the account of an ordinary soldier who fought—sometimes blindly and almost always fearfully—in a struggle that he never completely understood. The soldier, if he wants to live, learns how to fight and develops all sorts of little techniques that will keep him alive. He learns how to recognize signs of danger and how to react quickly to them. He learns to respect—and sometime fear—his enemy and he learns that the best way to keep himself from going off the deep end is to laugh and to find the humor in things that are anything but funny.

So consider this a survival manual, written by an infantry grunt who went through the battle and lived to share his experiences and the things that he learned.

This chapter, then, is where I try to share what I've learned in the sincere hope that it will be helpful to you in your struggles with bipolar disorder. Or to help you guide and assist a loved one who is struggling.

When I started writing this book, I thought of this as the "Self-Help Chapter." But, for some reason, I was never satisfied with that title. It seemed, somehow, anemic and bland. This is not a matter of losing weight or developing better social skills. It is, literally, a matter of life and death. We are not dealing, here, with a program for avoiding social embarrassment but ways of fighting off the urge to commit suicide.

I've finally started thinking of this as the "Self-Determination Chapter," because we're dealing with a struggle that will require from you all of your reserves of will and determination. You are in a hard fight. A very hard fight. One that will exhaust you and push you to the point where you feel like quitting. Without determination—and a lot of it—you will not win.

The first thing you must be determined to do is—face the truth. Denial is, initially, a natural reaction. Nobody wants to believe they are mentally ill. "It can't be," you say to yourself. "Not *me*."

This is understandable. More so, in my time when the stigma that came with mental illness was very real and very tough. These days, we are more enlightened. We know of famous people who have gone public as suffering from bi-polar. People like Ted Turner, the entrepreneur. Dick Cavett, the television personality. Buzz Aldrin, the astronaut. And many others.

So, these days, there isn't that heavy sense of stigmatization and shame that came with knowing you were bipolar. Still … nobody embraces the diagnosis when they first hear it.

Like I say, that initial reaction is understandable. Denial is almost instinctive. But eventually, you must get over it. You must admit the truth. And, as the lawyers, would have it—"the truth, the whole truth, and nothing but the truth." You must admit that you suffer from this disease and, just as important, you must admit that you cannot be "cured."

Denial always comes at a heavy—and sometimes fatal—price.

So, you are determined to accept the truth and face it squarely. No denial. What next?

Well, a couple of things. You need to get help. Believe me, you do not want to carry on this fight alone, the way I did for so many years. If you've been diagnosed, then you are already dealing with professionals and you can take the next step and ask to be referred to a doctor. If you haven't been diagnosed but suspect, from your symptoms, that you are bipolar, then get diagnosed.

The next step is to put yourself in the care of a doctor you trust and feel comfortable with. It took me a long time to find Gerry Kraines but when I did, at last, connect with him, it made all the difference in the world. If the first doctor you see doesn't "feel" right, then move on to another. This will be one of the most important relationships in your life. You must trust your doctor and there must be free and truthful communication between the two of you.

At the same time this is happening, you must become determined to fight your own fight. Being in the care of a good professional and taking whatever medications he prescribes is very important. But there is more to it. You are not simply a passenger along for the ride. Like I say, you are in a fight and you must be determined to fight back. Following your doctor's advice and taking your meds is, as the philosophers would put it, "necessary but not sufficient."

So, how do you fight back?

Well, in one way or another, that's what I've been writing about throughout this book. The fight is desperate—life and death, as I've said—but it is also very ordinary and prosaic. It can come down to something as basic as summoning the will to get out of bed.

Now, as a place to start, let's go with one of the basic rules of war: "Know your enemy."

As I said a few paragraphs back, there are many excellent books on the clinical nature of bipolar disorder. I've read several and I would recommend that you do this. Then, there are books that are more concerned with helping people deal with the everyday challenges the disease throws at them. There are two of these that I have found invaluable and that I have consulted many, many times over the years and that I revisit still.

The first of these books is *Mental Health Through Will-Training* by Dr. Abraham Low. The second is *Feeling Good* by Dr, David D. Burns.

I have written about a good deal about Dr. Low and his book and about *Recovery Inc.,* the program he founded that was such a help to me. His book was published in 1950. Dr. Burn's book was published in 1980 and it has been a tremendous success, worldwide, with, according to the publisher, "more than 3 million copies in print."

On his acknowledgements page, Dr. Burns writes:

"The development of cognitive therapy has been a team effort involving many talented individuals. In the 1930s, Dr. Abraham Low, a physician, began a free-of-charge self-help movement for individuals with emotional difficulties, called, "Recovery Incorporated," which is still in existence today. Dr. Low was one of the first health professionals to emphasize the important role of our thoughts and attitudes on our feelings and behavior. Although many people are not aware of his work, Dr. Low deserves a great deal of credit for pioneering many of the ideas that are in vogue today."

I have learned a lot from both books but I have also learned a lot on my own. And later, I would recognize the lessons that I learned—sometimes in slightly different form—in the pages of these books.

My reason for writing this book—one of them, anyway—is to share the lessons I have learned in the hope that they will be useful to others. They may be part of Dr. Low's program or they might be a part of what Dr. Burns calls "The New Mood therapy." For me, though, they are my lessons and I came by most of them the hard way. That's the way you will come by your lessons. Dr. Low and Dr. Burns will provide maps but you must walk the trail.

So what are the most important—and successful—techniques I've used for dealing with my condition?

The most basic is to recognize symptoms and understand them for what they are. Dr. Low called this "spotting." If you learn to recognize those things that push you into an emotionally dangerous place (Dr. Low called these "triggers") then you can force yourself to avoid them or detour around them. But this takes discipline and will power.

Cognitive therapy is built on discipline and will power.

Then, there are those occasions when there is no preventing an occurrence of the symptoms. You are in a state of depression and nothing you could have done would have prevented it. You need to be able to recognize this for what it is. It is a form of self-diagnosis. Of stepping a little outside of yourself and saying, "Okay. We know about this. We've been here before. Now, what do we do about it?"

This is critical. You have to believe that you can do something about your depression. That there are steps that you can take. If you believe that it is something that has simply overtaken you and that you can't do anything until it passes, then you may never get out of bed. One empty day will pass into another and each day of doing nothing will amplify your depression. You will fall into a state that Dr. Burns calls "do-nothingism."

The lesson, here, is that you must *do something*. And I mean anything. What I learned, before I'd been to my first meeting of *Recovery Inc.* and read the first words from Dr. Low's book, was that if I spent the day working on one of my wood carvings and at the end of the day, could point to a pile of shavings on the floor, *I felt better.*

Why? Because I had accomplished *something*. I could look at the shavings and look at the carving and I could tell myself that I had done that and that I was making progress on my project. And my real project, even if I didn't know it, was not the carving but *me*. I was working on myself. And little-by-little, I was making progress.

If you do nothing, you magnify your feeling of worthlessness. Allowing yourself to feel like you just *can't* do anything will magnify your feeling of helplessness. Enough days of that and you begin to feel like nothing will ever change and you magnify your feeling of hopelessness.

You must do something. Dr. Low's phrase for this was, "Move your muscles." Activity and projects get the mind off itself and give you something to feel good about. This, Dr. Low, called "endorsing yourself."

So what do I do to move my muscles?

Whatever. I keep a list of jobs. A lot of them of the unpleasant, tedious sort. Clean out the garage. Organize my tools. Take a load of junk to the dump. These are jobs that don't require any great mental effort but in doing them, you tend to lose yourself. It feels almost impossible to make myself get started and, then, an hour into the project and I'm not thinking about my own depression any longer but trying to figure out where to put some useless item that has been cluttering up my garage for the last six months.

It sounds very small and very prosaic. And … well, it is. But we need to remember that much of life is prosaic and tedious and that people with problems like severe depression tend to think that everything should be fraught with meaning and importance. But sometimes the garage just needs to be cleaned and cleaning it makes you feel good; gives you a reason to endorse yourself. One of Dr. Low's phrases was, "Drop the need to be exceptional." There is nothing exceptional about cleaning the garage. But its satisfactions can be undeniable.

I've told the story of how I once spent two days fighting off an episode of depression brought on by Christmas by decorating my house. And, man, did I decorate it. Two solid days of hanging lights and stringing boughs until, when it was finished, it looked like the storefront at Macy's.

And I felt fine. Or pretty close, anyway.

There is no job too menial or tedious or repetitive to do, especially if it gives you some relief. It just needs to be done and you need to do it.

But … what if you simply don't have the motivation?

This is one of the great errors in human thinking. We believe that motivation must precede action. That before we can do something, we must first feel like doing it.

Here, from Dr. Burn's book, is one of the most helpful insights I have ever come across. I have it underlined, heavily, in my copy of his book:

What, in your opinion comes first—motivation or action?

If you said motivation, you made an excellent, logical choice. Unfortunately, you're wrong. Motivation does not come first, action does! You have to prime the pump. Then you will begin to get motivated, and the fluids will flow spontaneously.

Individuals who procrastinate frequently confuse motivation and action. You foolishly wait until you feel in the mood to do something. Since you don't feel like doing it, you automatically put it off.

Your error is your belief that motivation comes first, and then leads to activation and success. But it is usually the other way around; action must come first, and the motivation comes later on.

That nails it. You cannot wait around for motivation to come, you must give it—and yourself—a push. And it can be hard. People who have suffered from depression know how hard it can be merely to get out of bed. But you must do it and it is easier to do it—and, say, to launch into the project of cleaning up the garage—if you know that the motivation will eventually come and that you will feel better. Maybe not great. But better.

Knowing something and then acting on that knowledge. In my experience, that is a fundamental element of cognitive therapy.

So I keep that list and when I've accomplished one of the jobs, I cross it off and I add another. And I save those jobs for my bad days.

Actually, I keep all kinds of lists. And not simply because I like order. I do it because by making a list and checking things off of it, I can see that I have actually accomplished something. That I have not wasted a day. It is another way of endorsing myself.

And I keep my books handy. Books like those written by Dr. Low and Dr. Burns. I have places in them where I have underlined passages and made notes in the margins. I keep going back to those books, and others, as another kind of discipline. This condition of mine will never go away so it is, logically, a subject that deserves lifetime of study. I read and reread the important texts. And I look for new books.

Reading in general is important. I like a good book. History, especially. As I've said, I like to read about Lincoln and Churchill. This kind of reading takes you out of yourself and that is both a relief and therapeutic. For some reason, watching television does not have the same effect. When I am depressed, a day of watching television just makes me feel worse.

I write letters. I don't know how to do e-mail and I don't have a cell phone and I suspect they wouldn't be good for me since they don't demand the kind of concentration and discipline that writing a letter does.

I try to exercise. Walking is a good way for me to move my muscles.

I go back, over and over, in my mind to the things I have learned. To the insights that have carried me through the worst times.

And I make myself remember a couple of sayings from Dr. Low that get, I think, to the most important lesson of all:

- We suffer from seriousness.
- A sense of humor is the sovereign means for curing nervous conditions.

Dr. Low also said, "Temper is your worst enemy. Humor is your greatest friend."

So I make myself remember that and I find ways to make myself laugh. I have dogs and they are great for that. And the friends I've made and kept over the years tend to be people, like me, who love a good laugh. It took me a while to learn it but I try consciously to find the humor in things and in myself, especially. My heroes, Lincoln and Churchill, were both great with humor and I believe it helped them not just survive but prosper.

There is a story a friend told me that I like and that seems to fit here. It is about a man who came home after spending more than five years as a POW in Vietnam. His plane had been shot down and he was badly injured and then tortured. Now he was home and one night he was at a party and someone found out about what he'd been through and kept asking him to describe the experience.

The man who'd been a POW kept trying to brush off the questions but the other man wouldn't let up. Finally the former POW said, "You know,

I'd like to help you out but I can't. You see, I'm afraid I only remember the funny parts."

It takes a real exercise of will to find the humor in things when you are depressed. But that is what cognitive therapy as all about. Recognizing the causes of your distress and then managing your thoughts and impulses and making yourself do the things that you know will help. And finding ways to keep your sense of humor.

It isn't magic. It is better than that.

CHAPTER 26

CHAPTER 26

After Gerry Kraines had diagnosed my condition and I had gone on medication, things changed. Of course they did. For one thing, I was not living a life of bluff and concealment any longer. I didn't broadcast my condition. No point in that. I still had a business to run and I didn't want to alarm possible clients who might not yet be enlightened about mental illness. But I told some people. They were, all of them, exceedingly surprised.

"You're not serious, Steve. I'd *never* have guessed."

The usual response went something like that. A few people seemed a little embarrassed for me. I didn't feel embarrassed at all. "Liberated" would be more like it.

Life was easier without the pressure that goes along with keeping a big secret. But I still had some bad times and still had need of all those lessons and techniques I have described in this book.

My friends all stayed with me. I continued to have trouble with women. Gerry Kraines left the practice of medicine and went on to his work in management studies and consulting. I went with a new doctor, William Jeanblanc who has been patient and insightful and as much a friend as a physician.

I knew when I started my business that I didn't want to run it until I was in the ground. There was more to life—not least hunting and fishing—and I wanted to enjoy those things while I was still able. So 20 years after starting with Diane in a room above the unemployment office, I sold the business to my employees. I actually helped with the financing and held on to the building I'd built.

The company has been sold again. But the building is still there and I still collect rent. At one time, when I still had the business, one out of every four people who lived in Peterborough was working there.

So with time on my hands, I traveled. To Argentina and Scotland for the hunting. Alaska and Labrador for the fishing. And to other places. I've split my year between South Carolina and the home I love in New Hampshire. A house that was built in 1780 and where I hang some of my most treasured collectables including a letter from Abraham Lincoln.

I am not cured and, as I've said many times in this book, I never will be. I still have my bad days. But I have made my peace and I have reached a point where I want to share some of the things I've learned. Maybe I can spare others some of the pain my learning those lessons caused me.

I still own the German Lugar. At one time, I would take it out and look at it and think about that night when I was ready to shoot myself with it. I did this fairly frequently, in fact. Did it, I'm sure, to remind myself of how close I'd come to destroying myself and how high the stakes were. I would look at the pistol and think about a lot of things.

But I haven't done that for a long, long time now.

And I doubt I ever will again.

STEPHEN MILLARD

BUY A SHARE OF THE FUTURE IN YOUR COMMUNITY

These certificates make great holiday, graduation and birthday gifts that can be personalized with the recipient's name. The cost of one S.H.A.R.E. or one square foot is $54.17. The personalized certificate is suitable for framing and will state the number of shares purchased and the amount of each share, as well as the recipient's name. The home that you participate in "building" will last for many years and will continue to grow in value.

Here is a sample SHARE certificate:

YES, I WOULD LIKE TO HELP!

I support the work that Habitat for Humanity does and I want to be part of the excitement! As a donor, I will receive periodic updates on your construction activities but, more importantly, I know my gift will help a family in our community realize the dream of homeownership. **I would like to SHARE in your efforts against substandard housing in my community!** *(Please print below)*

PLEASE SEND ME _____ SHARES at $54.17 EACH = $ $_____

In Honor Of: _____

Occasion: (Circle One)   HOLIDAY   BIRTHDAY   ANNIVERSARY

       OTHER: _____

Address of Recipient: _____

Gift From: _____ *Donor Address:* _____

Donor Email: _____

I AM ENCLOSING A CHECK FOR $ $_____ PAYABLE TO HABITAT FOR HUMANITY <u>OR</u> PLEASE CHARGE MY VISA OR MASTERCARD *(CIRCLE ONE)*

Card Number _____ Expiration Date: _____

Name as it appears on Credit Card _____ Charge Amount $ _____

Signature _____

Billing Address _____

Telephone # Day _____ Eve _____

PLEASE NOTE: Your contribution is tax-deductible to the fullest extent allowed by law.
Habitat for Humanity • P.O. Box 1443 • Newport News, VA 23601 • 757-596-5553
www.HelpHabitatforHumanity.org

LaVergne, TN USA
10 March 2011
219629LV00007B/62/P